From My Brother's
SHADOW

Oak of Acadiana Publications
18896 Greenwell Springs RD
Greenwell Springs, LA 70739
www.thepublishedword.com

Finally speaking out ...

From My Brother's

SHADOW

Teamster Doug Partin Tells His Side of the Story

by

Douglas Westley Partin

Published by:

Oak of Acadiana Publications
Greenwell Springs, LA 70739
www.thepublishedword.com

ISBN 978-1-934769-93-5
Trade Paper Version

Printed on demand in the US, the UK and Australia
For Worldwide Distribution

DEDICATION

To my wife, Sandra McCraine Wilbert Partin: without your urging, this book would have never been possible. Your unwavering support through the hard times and the good times these many married years has been my tower of strength, and my love for you is unending. May I continue to have the benefit of your counsel and strength and your undying love.

ACKNOWLEDGMENTS

My heartfelt thanks go out to my cousin Brenda McCurley White, for introducing me to my cousin-in-law, Sherrill Sue Britt McCurley. Sherrill, you were my motivation for telling my story and are among my most cherished and beloved people in the world. Your inspiration, dedication and contribution to this book were immense and, without you, I would have never told the story. I hope someday you will receive the recognition you deserve for your brilliant writing skills. You were a godsend. May God bless you and your beautiful family.

Special thanks to the Union Members of Teamsters Local #5: you were the best a union leader could have hoped for. All you ever wanted was to make a decent living for yourselves and your families, and it was the greatest privilege and honor to have represented you. I did my very best, even when sometimes that was not good enough. Thanks to each of you for the great honor you gave me through my years of service, and I wish each of you a long and healthy life.

Thanks to Frances Webb for your loyal support as a superb secretary and your friendship through the years. My very best wishes for your happiness and long life. May God be with you always.

Special thanks to my family members. Without them, this entire story would not have been. My brothers, Edward Grady Partin and Donald Lesley Partin, are now deceased. To my sisters, Hazel Elizabeth Partin Chancellor and Sandra Ann Foster Guy: I love you both very much.

To all my readers: I have told my story as I remembered it, through the good, the bad, the hurtful and the happy times. I hope you enjoy it and benefit from it in some way. Thank you, and may God bless you.

CONTENTS

PREFACE

Writing a book is no easy job. Before I attempted to write this one myself, I submitted a manuscript to another author and asked for their help. I was told that such an important work would first have to be thoroughly investigated and all details cleared before anything could be published. But the truth is that there *are* no documented sources for many of the things I am about to tell. Where newspaper or magazine articles exist, I have quoted them, but the problem is that newspapers and magazines could only print what Ed Partin wanted them to know, and usually that was just a fraction of the truth, or it was a complete fabrication altogether presented to them by Ed or his people to accomplish some personal goal of his. But I was there by his side and I saw and heard the things I am about to describe.

For the most part, there were no reporters present, no FBI agent to verify the details, nor any sheriff or district attorney to say it happened as I describe it here. Ed Partin was a very secretive man, and there were lots of things he didn't trust *me* to know. But he couldn't do everything himself, and when he needed help, he preferred to have family by his side. I was there, so what I am telling here is what I lived.

As I have written this book, looking back has sometimes affected me deeply and caused me some sleepless nights. If I could go back and change some of the things that were done, I would, but I can't. It happened, and it's time for a more complete story to be told.

INTRODUCTION

When I made the decision to step down from my position as leader of the Baton Rouge, Louisiana, local (Local #5) of the International Brotherhood of Teamsters Union in 1994, I made a public statement that I intended to write a book about my experiences. That made a lot of people nervous. After all, Local #5 had gained a reputation through the years of being one of the most ruthless unions in the nation.

That reputation was well deserved, for the union had been led for thirty years by my brother, Edward Grady Partin, a man who had no morals. Ed was Ed, and he felt like the world owed him something and that he could do what he wanted to do, when he wanted to do it, and take what he wanted, no matter who got hurt in the process. For many years, he seemed to get away with it, but then the long arm of the law finally caught up with him, and he spent many years in federal prison for his crimes.

Ed was otherwise famous for being the government's star surprise witness in the case against notorious Teamsters Boss Jimmy Hoffa in 1982, for "informing" federal agents about an alleged plot against the life of then Attorney General Bobby Kennedy, and for his connections to mob leaders, in New Orleans and around the country. He even had ties to Communist leaders like Fidel Castro and Huey Newton and once forged an arms deal with Castro. Ed would do anything for a buck.

Through the years, many books, newspapers and magazines have told stories about my brother, but as I read them I realized that they were either only partially true or total fabrications concocted by Ed himself and fed to press contacts who liked him and served his many interests. As someone who was there and witnessed it all, I knew. And I have decided that it is finally time to set the record straight and document the truth.

"Why now?" some have asked. Well, both Ed and my other brother, Donald, are gone now, so I can't do them any harm. I loved them both dearly and would not have done anything to hurt them while they were still alive. And, like all of us, I'm getting older, so I don't know how much longer I'll have to tell my story. It's time the truth were told.

For far too many years, my life was lived in the shadow of my older brother. From the time we were very small, he dominated us and could convince us to do almost anything he wanted. For our part, we idolized him and willingly gave him what he asked for. Part of this was instilled in us by our mother. Ed was her boy. She felt that he could do no wrong and always encouraged us to cooperate with him. But, even beyond the family circle, Ed had always been a very charming guy, and everyone liked him and responded to him. The amazing thing is that even when Ed abused his friends and family, as he often did, everyone continued to like him. This was true throughout his life. I, personally, loved him to the very end.

Looking back on it now, I suppose it was only Ed's legal misfortunes that allowed me to finally step out of his shadow and start to make a name for myself. It was Ed who first appointed me as principal officer of Local #5 (because he was being imprisoned on charges of conspiracy to obstruct justice). Later, when I had decided to retire, it was Ed who came to me and begged me to return to that position. And yet, Ed trusted no one (me included) and often sought to undermine me, even putting out contracts on my life.

As much as I loved Ed, I never understood him or why he did the things he did. Often they made no sense at all. It was just Ed being Ed.

There were many things that went on during Ed's time as boss of Local #5 that I am not proud of at all. I was there by his side and was often involved in his shenanigans. Even if I wasn't involved, for he was also very secretive and many of those closest to him never knew the details of his private doings (for instance, his money), I was always suspected, along with him, simply because I was his younger brother and had served him for so many years.

Through all those troublesome years, as I was observing how things were being done wrong, I was also thinking about how they could be done right and how much better that would be for everyone concerned. So, when my time came to run the union, I began immediately to implement the needed reforms, and I led the local with honesty and integrity for many years after Ed had lost control.

For far too many years, that huge shadow was always there, often in a very threatening way, but I had learned that I could live free of it, and I did. Ed hated me for that, and when I visited him moments before he died, I sensed that Ed had very bad feelings for me. But I still loved him just as much as ever. This is my story.

Doug Partin

WHAT IS THE
TEAMSTERS UNION?

My story is also the story of the Teamsters Union, particularly Local #5 in Baton Rouge, Louisiana, for I worked with the Teamsters, in one capacity or another, for forty-five years, my brother Ed led the Baton Rouge local for thirty years, and I succeeded him, retiring in 1994.

Most of those who lived through the 1950s and 60s will understand more what it meant to be a Teamster, for the unions in that period — the Teamsters included — were more a part of everyday American life, and the sometimes rough goings-on in union activities (organizing workers and conducting picket lines and strikes to gain workers their rights) often dominated newspaper and magazine headlines. This was especially true during the time of Teamsters boss Jimmy Hoffa, which was the same period of the reign of my brother Ed in the Baton Rouge area.

The younger generations of Americans, however, are not nearly as familiar with the history of unions in this country because the influence of unions has declined. So allow me take a few paragraphs to explain what the Teamsters are all about.

The Teamsters, known officially by their longer name, the International Brotherhood of Teamsters Union, had its roots in colonial times, when men who drove horse-drawn wagons formed the backbone of North American development. Despite their essential role, however, as guardians of trade — the lifeblood of the economy — these men were often exploited. Sometimes work was scarce, jobs were insecure, and poverty was commonplace among men who did this work and the families that depended on them.

According to the Teamsters official website (www.teamster.org), in 1900 the typical teamster worked twelve to eighteen hours a day, seven days a week, for an average wage of just $2 a day. On top of that, a teamster (or driver, in our modern terms) was expected not only to haul his load, but also to assume liability for bad accounts and for lost or damaged merchandise. So the teamsters were left assuming all of the risks and with little chance for serious reward.

In 1901, frustrated and angry drivers banded together to form the Team Drivers International

Union (TDIU), with an initial membership of 1,700. The following year, some of those members broke away and formed a rival group, the Teamsters National Union. In 1903 the two groups agreed to rejoin forces in what was now called the International Brotherhood of Teamsters.

The goal of the Teamsters from the first day was to represent the working men and women of North America who played such a crucial role in the growth of industrialization and the transportation that fueled it. The struggles and triumphs of these men and women would shape the economic, class and social trends in America more than any other group. The Teamsters fought for the rise of North America's working families into the middle class, the empowerment of workers through collective bargaining and on-the-job protections for health, safety and retirement security, becoming a powerful voice for the dignity of workers and their workplace.

As America grew, the Teamsters went on to represent far more than wagon drivers. Although truck drivers continued to be a sizable part of union membership, the union also represented a large number of construction workers, but also workers of every type — even public service workers. In representing laundry workers, the Teamsters was the first union to insist on equal pay for blacks as for whites. This dedication to the equal pay principle continues to this day. The Teamsters came to play such a dominant role in the American workplace in past decades that some have called the 20th Century the Teamster Century.

That unnecessary violence, greed and corruption entered the picture, especially in the 1950s and 60s, was a sad note that cannot be ignored in Teamsters history. Many Teamsters officials of that period, including my own brother, were convicted of crimes and served time in prison for those crimes. This, of course, included Jimmy Hoffa (who was convicted on the testimony of my brother, a fellow Teamster.)

The national organization of Teamsters is made up of many local organizations. My story includes two of those locals: the Natchez, Mississippi, local, which was started by my brother Ed, and the Baton Rouge local, which he led for some thirty years, before I succeeded him in that role. When I assumed the leadership of the Baton Rouge local, I started cleaning house and rid Local #5 of its corrupt practices, serving the working men and women of the Baton Rouge area with dignity and respect.

Within a local union, the leadership consists of

a principal officer, or boss (officially called the Secretary-Treasurer/Business Manager), a president (the second in command), an advisory board, and a group of assistant business agents. If the local can afford it, the principal officers are paid a salary. Assistant business agents often work as volunteers, receiving only the reimbursement of expenses made in carrying out their duties on behalf of the union.

Keeping these simple facts in mind should help to explain my story.

CHAPTER 1

OUR BEGINNINGS

In the year 1930, on April 17th, I was born to Grady Edward Partin and Mary Elizabeth "Bessie" Mathis Partin, the youngest of their four children. My mother gave me the name Douglas Westley Partin.

At the time of my birth, home was a simple shotgun house located in a small country community known as Buffalo Hill in Wilkinson County, Mississippi. The house had newspaper covering the inside walls. Mother mixed flour and water to make a paste and then used that paste to glue the newspaper over the holes and cracks in the walls to keep the cold wind out during the wintertime.

From My Brother's Shadow

My dad worked for Netterville Sawmill, which was just about the only place in the area at the time that one *could* work for a decent wage. But Daddy liked to drink, and he liked to gamble. Between paydays, sawmill employees were allowed to charge at the company store, and Daddy took full advantage of that privilege. When payday rolled around and the accumulated charges were deducted from his pay, very little, if anything, was left. There were some paydays when he would receive an empty pay envelope, and there were times when he received an envelope showing that he still owed the company store after all his pay had been deducted.

Sawmill employees were paid in cash, after deductions, and some of the men, my Daddy among them, got in the habit of gathering outside the mill after work every payday to gamble and drink together. The result was that Daddy often came home on paydays penniless and drunk, to a wife and four children who were hungry and in need of clothing. This went on for years, and during that time, we had practically nothing. But, because we children were still small, we didn't realize how poor we were. We thought everyone lived that way.

There were days when we had no food at all in the house, and I remember my mother taking us around to a neighbor's house just at suppertime and dropping us off, hoping we would be invited inside and be offered something to eat.

Sometimes I would spend the night at my aunt's house. None of my other siblings liked to spend the night there because they knew the only place to sleep was with her youngest son, and he had the habit of wetting the bed. I didn't care because I knew I would get something to eat and not have to go to bed hungry. I might not sleep well that night, but I surely wouldn't be hungry again.

I remember us moving on one occasion just to have access to some food. A neighbor just up the road had recently moved away and had left a turnip green garden in the back yard. We transferred to that house just to get those greens.

As I look back, however, I don't ever remember thinking about being poor. As children we didn't realize we were going through such hard times. To us, it was simply the way of life at the time. After all, those were the early years of the Great Depression.

I guess I was about three when my mother had finally had enough of the drinking, gambling and abuse. Daddy came home one particular night, drinking as usual, and came in the door of that little shotgun house with a gallon of syrup in his hand. Then, for some reason, he took the lid off of it and began pouring the syrup out all over the floor as he walked through the house. He kept pouring until the container was empty. All we could do, our mother and four hungry children, was to watch helplessly. Our stomachs were empty, and that syrup had been the only relief in sight.

Mother left that night and never came back. She slipped away sometime during the night, leaving us four children behind. It was the end of their marriage.

Mother had first met my father in 1922. Her father, Raleigh J. Mathis, came to Wilkinson County, Mississippi, to work at the sawmill, alongside the Partin men, and he brought my mother, Bessie, with him. My grandfather and my mother remained on the Partin property for about two weeks and, during that time, the Partin girls became well acquainted with my mother and decided she should marry their brother, Grady Edward. Life must have been hard for Mother because she agreed to the marriage, even though she didn't love Grady, and they were married on May 27, 1922.

After Mom and Dad were married, they lived on the Partin property and Mom was taken advantage of by the Partins in every way imaginable. I assume she had thought about her young life for years and realized how hard it had been, but this life certainly wasn't any easier. Later on, after I was a grown man, Mother told me that she had served the Partins as a washwoman, a cook and anything else they needed her services for. It wasn't much of a life.

Mother and Grady had four children, one after the other. She later told close family members that she had never loved Grady, and she told me the same thing. It was a kind of arranged marriage, she said, and pressure had been put on her to marry Daddy. But she did have four children by him, so I never could discern if she had really loved him at some point or not. Who's to say?

What I do know is that when she left us that night of the syrup incident, she went to Natchez, Mississippi, where a friend took her in. Her intention was to save her sanity, but also to make a new life for herself and her four children. She later filed for divorce from our father and sent for us one by one.

When Mother first arrived in Natchez, she took a job at the box factory there, working five days a week. In those days boxes were made from wood, and she assembled the various precut pieces. She also worked a half day on Saturdays at Kress' Five and Dime Store, and she took in sewing and worked odd jobs to make extra money as well. I was told that she sewed curtains for some of the famous antebellum homes in Natchez. Mother was a fantastic seamstress and continued sewing and quilting until she was in her late eighties.

When Mother finally felt she had saved enough money, she began sending for us children. Since I was the youngest, she sent for me first. It was April of 1933, so I was still three. She next sent for one of my older brothers, Donald, who was five at the time. My sister Hazel had been living with an aunt, but she came to Natchez to live with us in time to enroll in grade school. And then there was Ed ...

Ed was the oldest of the children, senior to me by seven years. He was a big, strong, handsome young man, and everyone liked him. The other three of us were little red-headed freckle-faced children that no one really wanted. Ed was always the star of the show, and he did what he wanted to do when he wanted to do it.

For instance, Ed was always allowed the freedom to go and come as he pleased. He could stay with Daddy, come live with us, or live anywhere else he wanted. Most of the time he chose to stay in Wilkinson County with the Partin and Priest families, where he was well taken care of and had most everything he wanted and/or needed.

Sometimes, when he felt like it, Ed would come to Natchez and stay with us, but when he did, there was always trouble. He would either cause us trouble or get himself into some kind of trouble. Ed was trouble.

After the divorce became final, on September 13, 1932, Daddy moved out of state, to Clinton, Louisiana, to avoid paying Mother any child support. He had found work at a saw mill there owned by Monroe Hatcher. For some reason, I wound up there with him for a while when I was four or five. All three of us boys were there: Ed, Donald and I. As young as I was, I remember the place well. It was very near the mill, and there was a cemetery close by.

I remember that place most for two things: One, Mother came to town one day, either to see us boys or to try to take us back to live with her in Natchez. When she got to the house where we were staying, we were nowhere to be found. She finally found us ... in a local bar with Daddy. He was drunk and had Donald sitting on top of the bar. When he saw Mother coming in the barroom door, he picked Donald up and put him out the barroom window.

Mother saw him do it, and raised hell. To this day, I'm not sure why Daddy did that.

The other thing I remember is that during the time we stayed with Daddy in Clinton, he had a maid who came in every morning to take care of us boys. Every day she cooked homemade biscuits for us, and we ate them with syrup, but Donald and I could never have any until Ed had eaten all he wanted. We then ate what was left over. Sometimes, when there was nothing left, Donald and I had to do without. At that early age, Ed already had his hold on us.

After we were reunited in Natchez, Mother, Donald, Hazel and I struggled along as a family (with Ed's occasional visits). We were poor, but at least we were together.

As poor as we were, I knew how to get my candy. I always came up with little money-making schemes and, when I did, I would spend all the money I made on candy. Oh, how I loved my candy.

Let me tell you about one of my more successful schemes: I would go down to the train depot on Canal Street in Natchez at about the time the railroad workers were due to come back from their day's labor and play on their sympathies. Men who were hoping to find work on the railroad would gather there at the depot early in the morning. Trucks came along and picked out from them those who would be hired for the day and took them to the areas where their services were needed. Then, in the evening, when the day's work had ended, those workers were returned to the same location. Sometimes it was getting dark or already dark when they returned.

I would be sitting on the steps of the train depot waiting for them, and when they arrived, I would cry and pretend to be lost and upset. Some of the men fell for it and would feel sorry for me and give me nickels and pennies. No sooner had they placed those coins in my little hand than I would run as fast as I could to the candy store.

On one of those candy-money-seeking visits to the train depot, a man came up to me, as I was pretending to cry, picked me up in his arms and asked me where I lived. I didn't want to tell him where I lived and have him take me home. All I wanted was a nickel or a penny for some candy. He insisted and took me home that evening anyway and, as a result, met my mother. That man, Thomas Andrew Foster, later became my step-father.

Mother married Mr. Foster, not because she was in love with him, but in order to give her children a better life. And that she did. She also gave Andrew a child, a daughter, Sandra Ann Foster, born on May 3, 1945.

Donald and I considered ourselves lucky to have Andrew as a father and felt that he really loved us. He was a good man, and I appreciated him. I had never really known a real daddy before until I knew him. What's the old saying? "Any man can be a father, but it takes someone special to be a daddy."

Andrew later took a job at Armstrong Tire and Rubber Company in Natchez and moved the family to 513 North Union Street. It was a two-story house, and we lived upstairs. The family downstairs eventually moved, and we moved downstairs. It was a very nice area of Natchez to grow up in.

Things began to quickly change as I got older, and before long I learned to work and earn for myself. I picked up pecans in the fall and sold them to the local pecan factory. I picked figs when they were in season and sold them, for fifty cents a gallon without stems and twenty-five cents a gallon with stems. I had regular customers along North Union Street who would buy them from me every year. Mother and I would pick a foot tub of figs early every morning, and then I would make my rounds up and down the street yelling "figs for sale."

I also had a daily paper route and would sell the

local newspaper on the street every Sunday. I was able to buy two Sunday papers for a nickel and turn around and sell them for a nickel each. Even though I was about twelve at the time, I walked the streets of my neighborhood barefoot selling figs or newspapers. I had no shoes, and that fact embarrassed me. I can still remember the slap-slap sound of my bare feet hitting against the concrete. It seemed that everyone else in Natchez had shoes except me.

But life was getting better, and I was growing up, and as I did, I found all types of interesting ways to make money. Somewhere in my early teens, I discovered how to be an effective go-between for lonely soldiers and the women of our local "cathouses." There was an army base called Camp Van Dorn located just outside Centreville, Mississippi (about forty miles from Natchez), and some forty thousand troops were stationed there. In Natchez, there were three houses that catered to the carnal needs of these men. All three houses were owned and run by black women, but the working girls were of many different races.

One of those houses was called Big Mama's and was located on Broadway Street, next door to a grocery store. Another was called Annie Wise's Place, and the third one was called Nellie Jackson's Place.

From My Brother's Shadow

Nellie's Place was located on Rankin Street, and Annie's Place was in the ally next to Nellie's. That ally was near our house, and it seems to me that Rankin Street was just one street over behind North Union Street, where we lived.

I would search out the Army men when they came into Natchez and ask them if they wanted a woman. If they said yes, then I led them to Nellie's place, and Nellie would tell them to give me a quarter for my trouble in bringing them there. Nellie would feed me too, and it was good food, like rice and beans, pork, sausage and fried chicken. I found her to be a very fine person, and she was always good to me.

I led the soldiers up Nellie's driveway and into her back door and then showed them where to sit on the sofa to await their turn. I sat there with them. When it came their turn to go in and do their business with the girls, Nellie would bring me a plate of food, and I would sit there and eat it as I waited for the soldiers to come back out. When the soldiers were ready to go, Nellie would tell them to tip me a quarter, and if they didn't, she would give me a quarter herself.

As I matured, our brother Ed continued his visits to Natchez — if and when he had the urge. He would arrive like the wind and have his way with everything and everybody and then leave just as suddenly as he had arrived. I can never forget one particular instance (that happened at an earlier time).

Mother had had an accident while getting off of a bus and had hurt her back and, as a result, came into a little money through an insurance settlement. She bought Donald and me new tricycles. Because Ed was older, she bought him some nice clothes she thought he would like and appreciate. As it turned out, Ed neither liked nor appreciated the clothes, and, instead, he became very angry and upset.

Donald and I were out in the middle of North Union Street in front of our house, riding our new tricycles, and Ed came out of the house, tore our tricycles up and beat the hell out of the two of us. He was jealous because Mother had bought us tricycles and had bought him clothing. As usual, Mother overlooked the whole incident and never said a word to Ed about his actions.

Then, as the years progressed, Ed began stealing from Mother. She bought herself a car, and he stole it. In an effort to keep it out of his hands, she kept her car keys hidden under her pillow on her bed, but he found them. He wrecked the car and totaled it. She used the insurance money from that wreck to replace the vehicle, but Ed stole the second car and wrecked it, too.

This time Mother didn't replace the car and, instead, spent the next twelve years without a vehicle because she knew her errant son would just do the same thing again.

Ed also stole from our step-father Andrew. Andrew would buy new suits to wear to church on Sunday, and Ed would steal them and sell them to get cash for his personal pursuits. Still, Ed could do no wrong in Mother's eyes. He constantly bullied us younger children, but when he gave us orders, we obliged him, because he was our older brother and we looked up to him and would do anything and everything he asked us to. He had some sort of hold over us. This was especially true of me.

One evening Ed said he needed my help with something and asked me to go with him. He didn't tell me where we were going or what we were going to do, but I didn't resist and, instead, tagged along with my big brother. He took me downtown to Franklin Street. More specifically, we went to 509 Franklin Street. It was the location of Feltus Brothers Hardware Store. Ed had me climb up with him onto the roof of the store. He then tied a rope around my waist and lowered me down through the skylight into the store. Once I was inside, he called down for me to tie the rope around a gun that was for sale, and I followed his instructions. After he had hauled out that gun, he had me tie it around gun after gun, and he pulled them each up separately onto the roof. I don't remember how many guns Ed pulled out of the hardware store that night, but I know it was a bunch. Other than Sears, Roebuck and Company, Feltus Brothers Hardware was about the only place in Natchez that sold guns at the time, and Ed was helping himself to many of the guns they currently had in stock.

Eventually I saw a BB gun I wanted and started tying it to the rope so that Ed could pull it out for me, but he told me I couldn't have it. I wanted that BB gun, and I told Ed I wasn't coming up without it. We argued for a while, but he eventually pulled me out with the BB gun in my hands.

Not long afterward, Ed began selling those stolen guns. He made a trip to New Orleans to sell some and was still in New Orleans when the local police came to our house and began to question us. They asked Mother's permission to search the house for stolen guns. Of course she didn't know anything about the guns, so she willingly gave them permission to search. In the attic they found the remainder of the guns which had not yet been sold. Ed was in major trouble.

I was questioned by the police about the incident, and I told them exactly what Ed and I had done. We were both required to go to court over the matter. I was put on the witness stand and questioned in court, and I told them exactly, in detail, what we had done. As a consequence, no formal charges were filed against me, but Ed was sent to reform school.

I remember going with Mother to visit Ed and take him food, and I also remember the benches outside the building where we would sit while Mother visited him and he ate the food she had brought him from home.

Ed remained in reform school for a while, until he was offered a release, but one of the conditions for that release was that he agree to join the Marines. He felt he had no choice, so he agreed, but his stay in the Marines was cut short by his continued unacceptable conduct. He received a dishonorable discharge, I believe because of theft. (He told us it was because he had assaulted an officer). Later in life, Ed used some of his connections to get this "dishonorable discharge" changed to an "undesirable discharge." Meanwhile, I was still the hard-working young man with the newspaper route.

Our Beginnings

Then I got *myself* in trouble. An old man who lived near us there in Natchez had a Cushman motor scooter, and he wanted to sell it for $250. The scooter had a sidecar on it, and I could just see myself delivering newspapers around town using that scooter, with the newspapers in the sidecar.

I approached my mother and ask her if I could buy it. She, of course, didn't have money to buy it, but she told me that if I would work and save money, I could buy it myself. I continued selling newspapers and figs, along with my other money-making schemes, and gave all the money I made to Mother to save for me, until I was sure I had enough to buy the scooter. I knew exactly how much money I had saved up because I had kept up with every dime I had given Mother to set aside. It was now $250, and I really wanted that scooter to run my paper route. I was going to be a big wheel in Natchez, riding that scooter through the streets, with my newspapers loaded in the sidecar.

So now I went to Mother and told her that I was ready to buy the scooter. I was devastated to hear her say that I would not be able to get the scooter because she had spent the money. Oh, how that hurt! I had worked so hard, delivering newspapers, picking and selling figs and doing many other things, to earn all that money, and now this.

This happened somewhere in the mid 1940s, when I was fifteen or sixteen. I had some friends my age, and now several of those friends and I decided to go to the house of the old man who owned the scooter and just take it for a ride. What harm could come from that? In my hurt state, I wasn't thinking very clearly. So I hopped on the scooter and took it for a ride around Natchez.

Since Natchez is just across the river (the mighty Mississippi) from Vidalia, Louisiana, I went across the bridge, crossing the state line from Mississippi into Louisiana, and before long, I was stopped by the Louisiana authorities. Since I had no papers, I was arrested and put in jail, and soon I was transported to a jail in New Orleans.

When I arrived in New Orleans, I was questioned as to what my name was, and because I refused to tell the authorities anything, they kept me. They put me in a cell on the second floor, a large open room with about twenty men in it. I was just a young kid, and young boys were being raped in that room.

Every day the authorities took me downstairs for questioning and would ask if I was ready to talk to them about who I was. By the third day I was ready to tell them anything they wanted to know. I told them my name and where I lived and that I wanted to go home.

My step-father, Andrew Foster, was somehow notified, and he came to New Orleans to get me. But while he was there in the Crescent City, the poor man was robbed, and everything he had on him was taken.

He somehow gained my release, and we decided that the two of us would ride the scooter back to Natchez and started the trip back. Before long, we saw that this had not been a good idea. It was very slow going. Somehow he located someone with a pickup truck willing to load the scooter in the back and drive us back to Natchez. But we had no money to pay him.

Poor Andrew! He had come all the way to New Orleans to get me out of jail, had been robbed and now had to contact my Mother and have her send money so that we could get home.

Although Mother never told me so, I believe in my heart that she had spent the money I saved for the scooter on Ed and his legal problems. He stayed in trouble all the time and cost her plenty in fines and legal fees.

Or maybe she just gave him the money. She did that sometimes. She never told me she was sorry for spending the money, and she never gave me any kind of explanation as to where the money had gone or what it was used for. Sad to say, she was a selfish type of person, and she and her wants, needs and wishes always came before those of her children. Come to think of it, maybe that's where Ed got his troublesome nature.

I came to realize at a very early age that Ed was Mother's favorite, her pet, and he could do no wrong in her eyes. Little did I know that this was only the beginning of living the majority of my adult life in the shadow of this older brother, Edward Grady Partin.

CHAPTER 2

PERSONAL CHOICES

At the tender age of sixteen, I was now in some serious trouble of my own over that motor scooter incident. Charges had been filed against me, and I was required to appear in court before a judge. Because of my actions, I was forced, at that very early age, to make some important decisions regarding my future. This whole business was a frightening experience for me, and I didn't ever want to repeat it.

That day the judge sentenced me to three years probation for what I had thought, at the time, was an innocent joy ride on a motor scooter. Was I ever mistaken! The entire episode taught me a very important lesson: never take anything that doesn't belong to you. Period!

When the judge sternly delivered my sentence, he added that if I could manage to stay out of trouble for the next three years, there would be no permanent record of the whole motor scooter incident against me. I would have a clean slate. So I now had a choice to make, an all-important decision.

I felt that if I remained in Natchez, around the same old circumstances and the same people, I would find trouble again, or it would surely find me. So that day I made a very difficult decision; I decided that the best thing for me to do was to go into military service for the next three years. If I could do that, I could have a clean record when I returned home. That's what the judge had told me. So I enlisted in the United States Air Force in January of 1947, just a couple of months before my seventeenth birthday. Since I was still underage, Mother signed the necessary papers for me.

I remained in the United States Air Force for the next three years and was stationed first in San Antonio, Texas, and then, later, in Wichita Falls, Texas. During those three years, every month I purchased a twenty-five-dollar war bond and sent them all home to Mother to keep for me until I returned. My intention was to buy myself a car when I got out.

I received an honorable discharge from the United States Air Force on December 9, 1949, with the rank of corporal, and returned home to Natchez to total chaos. Ed had gotten in trouble again, and this time it was worse and would require jail time. He had been arrested on several different charges, including grand larceny, robbery with the use of a firearm and rape. The following article, of which I have a copy, appeared in a Woodville, Mississippi, newspaper, *The Woodville Republican*, on August 6, 1948. It read as follows:

> Edward Partin, who is being held without bond awaiting the action of the Wilkinson County Grand Jury in October, was moved last week to the Natchez jail, according to Sheriff Green B. Morris.
> Partin was arrested here in May and was charged with robbery with firearms and rape. He was moved to the Jackson jail on June 15, where he remained until last week.

Ed had two Natchez attorneys representing him on these charges, and I suppose Mother had retained the attorneys, because all hopes I had of buying myself that car when I returned home from the service were now gone. She had spent everything I had sent home during those three years, and I had nothing to show for all my hard work.

Donald had enlisted in the service about two years prior to my enlistment, and he, too, had been purchasing war bonds and sending them home to Mother for safekeeping. Like me, when he returned home from the service, he found that his bonds had also been cashed and spent. Once again Ed had taken precedence over everything and everyone else.

Donald and I both loved our brother very much and would have helped him in any way we possibly could, but I had just spent three years of my life trying to make things better for myself and had to return home to these sad circumstances. I was hurt again, and I was very angry over the situation Ed had put the entire family in. As a matter of fact, when I got home and discovered that every penny I had sent home had been spent, Ed and I ended up in a pretty good fight inside our house.

The result of the fight was that Ed whipped me good. At the time I weighed about a hundred and forty pounds, and Ed weighed about two hundred and forty-five pounds, so it wasn't much of a competition. And Ed being Ed, he never let me forget that whipping. For years afterward, his acquaintances would tell me the story that they had been told by him, of how he had beaten my ass.

Ed was something. He had always gotten whatever he wanted in life, and he seemed to feel that the entire world was there for him, and if he wanted something, he should be able to just take it. Sadly, he went on to live much of his life with that attitude, until it would no longer work for him. But it took many years for him to come to that realization.

The rape that he was accused of reportedly happened on May 1, 1948. He was indicted for it by a grand jury, and his trial was scheduled to begin on October 15. I was in Texas, serving my three years in the Air Force when he allegedly committed these crimes and was arrested for them, and I had not been in contact with him from the time I enlisted until I returned to Natchez in December of 1949. In the meantime, he had put our family through hell, as usual. Mother took care of everything for him, as she had always done, and Ed emerged from the entire situation smelling like a rose.

The rape case itself resulted in a hung jury. Many years later, I was told by a barber who cut my hair that he was the one who had hung the jury, and he told me he just couldn't see a white man going to jail for raping a black woman. That's exactly how he had said it. I have copies of the ballots turned in by the jurors, including a copy of this man's ballot, with his name on it, voting "not guilty." That man is deceased now but has living relatives. Most all of these documents are accessible to anyone at the Wilkinson County, Mississippi, Courthouse. I found them there myself late in the summer of 2006.

By the time I got home from the Air Force, Ed was working at the International Paper Company in Natchez. The mill was under construction at the time, and there were jobs to be had there, so both Donald and I took advantage of that opportunity and also went to work at the mill. Ed had married a girl whose brother-in-law was a superintendent at International Paper Company, and that's how he got *his* job at the mill.

Some problems arose at the mill when there were not enough truck drivers. There was no Teamsters Union in Natchez at the time, so Ed started one, and we all joined. As a matter of fact, we struck the International Paper Company for a while during the construction of the mill in the late 1940s to early 1950s. Somehow Ed managed to shut down the construction because of the driver shortage. He also managed to get some truck drivers hired. I was not a truck driver; I was a millwright's helper.

The principal officer for the Teamsters Union Local #5 in Baton Rouge, Louisiana, heard how Ed had handled the truck driver situation at the Natchez mill. His name was Paul Kuhns, and he was so impressed with what Ed had done that he came to Natchez and persuaded Ed to go to work for him in Baton Rouge.

Paul Kuhns was a good man, and many people, through the years, described him to me as "a mighty fine person." Paul hired Ed as an assistant business agent with Teamsters Local #5, and Ed worked in that position for about a year before he suddenly took over as boss of the local, becoming, at a very young age, its Secretary-Treasurer/Business Manager.

And I do mean "took over." During the year that Ed served as assistant business agent, he was sometimes sent out on jobs, but he also spent a lot of time hanging around the union hall. During that time, he stole many union records, and in those records he discovered some things that had not been done legally and proceeded to use this ill-gained knowledge to his personal benefit.

How did he do that? He took those records in his

hand, marched into his boss' office and told him that if he didn't resign his position with the union local, he would take the records to the U.S. Labor Department. Needless to say, his boss resigned; he did not want to lose his pension, which would have been the result if he had been fired rather than re-signing. I don't know personally what was in those records or what information exactly Ed was holding over his boss, but whatever it was, it was enough to force the man to resign.

Later on in life, I had the opportunity to meet Paul Kuhns' son. I had a long talk with him and told him exactly what my brother had done to force his father out of his position and how sorry I was for it.

With the competition out of the way, Edward Grady Partin could now take over, and that's what he did, assuming a position he would hold for many years to come and which he would use ruthlessly to reach his personal goals — whatever they happened to be at the moment.

From that time on, Ed didn't have to worry about running for or being elected to that office, as every-one else did. He made sure his union officers were handpicked by him, and when it came time for nominations for the union officers, he would posi-tion his thugs and bullies around, inside and outside the union hall, armed with large sticks and guns. They had orders from Ed to harass and intimidate the members as they came in.

The constitution of the International Brotherhood of Teamsters Union stated that nominations for officers would be made and then, thirty days after those nominations were made, an election would be held. Teamsters Local #5 had its nominations all right, and it had its election, but if Ed and his boys thought someone who showed up at the polls was against someone he wanted in office or if he wanted to make a change in a certain office, then his thugs and bullies went into action. They frightened the Teamsters members to death as they were coming in, and they would be so nervous they didn't know what to do. As a result, there was seldom anyone elected to the leadership of Local #5 that Ed didn't want elected. Ed was really something. He had punks working for him that would do anything to keep their jobs.

While all of these happenings were going on in Baton Rouge, I was busy in Natchez. I continued my work at International Paper Company, and I was also a member of the local Mississippi Army National Guard. On December 18, 1950, I was called up by the United States Army to active duty with

From My Brother's Shadow

Company B, 155th Infantry, Dixie Division, and I served in Korea for the next twelve months. And in 1951, I got married to Ruby Lucille Rushing.

After returning home from Korea, I remained in the Army Reserve/National Guard of the State of Mississippi and was appointed Second Lieutenant, Infantry, on May 19, 1957. I was eventually honorably discharged from the Armed Forces of the United States of America on November 16, 1960, and was very proud to have served my country.

While working at the plant, serving in the National Guard and starting my family, I was also furthering my eduction. I first attended Copiah-Lincoln Junior College in Wesson, Mississippi, and then Whitworth College in Brookhaven, Mississippi. This had to be done at night, after work.

The roads, in those days, were very old and winding between Natchez and the Brookhaven-Wesson area. It was approximately seventy-eight miles one way from Natchez to Wesson, and there were seven of us who made the trip back and forth together each evening. We would work all day, travel to Copiah-Lincoln for school every evening after work, return home around midnight that night and then get up early the next morning and go to work again.

Personal Choices

We all went as far as we could go with our education at Copiah-Lincoln Junior College and then enrolled at Whitworth College in Brookhaven. The daily drive to Brookhaven was sixty-five miles. It was a difficult time, but we toughed it out because we were thinking seriously of our future.

The difficult choice I had made as a teenager, to enter the Air Force, had proven to be a good one, and I had been seriously considering making a career of the military, but now I had a change of heart — with a little coaxing from brother Ed.

I was doing fine, working at International Paper Company, going to school at night and growing my family, but now Ed came to Natchez on several occasions and asked me to come to work for him in Baton Rouge with the union. He made it sound very appealing, but each time I told him "No."

I had been battling with the question of whether to continue working at the mill or go on to make a career of the military, and now Ed added to that dilemma whether or not to go to Baton Rouge and work alongside him. It took him a few visits to Natchez to convince me. He was all but begging me to come. In the end, he made it look so good, as he was gifted to do. He told me how well I could do, how we would be working together, and so on.

From My Brother's Shadow

Ed had also talked with Mother about my coming to work with him and asked her to try to persuade me to do it. Between the two of them constantly trying to influence my decision, I finally gave in and agreed to join him in Baton Rouge. I felt proud to be going to work for and with my brother. Little did I know what I was getting myself into.

The choice I made that day totally changed my life. The years ahead were filled with hurt, breach of trust and exposure to danger. There were some good times; I can't deny that. But the bad far outweighed the good.

I joined Ed with the Teamsters Local #5 in the mid 1950s. I was just twenty-five years old, and he hired me as an assistant business agent, and I began learning the ropes in the union. Later our brother Donald moved to Baton Rouge and joined us, so there were three of us brothers in the local. Donald always worked in the field, never in the union hall.

Because I was not yet on the union payroll, I got a job at Kaiser Aluminum in Baton Rouge (and continued to work there for several years) and, of course, I became a proud member of Teamsters Local #5. At the same time I was employed with Kaiser, I was doing my work as assistant business agent. Although I was not on the payroll, I was reimbursed by the union for any expenses I incurred as a result of my union business. Kaiser was very good about allowing me to take off from work, if I needed to, in order to take care of union business.

One of the first things I did for the union was to work alongside Ed setting up picket lines and organizing new members for the union. I did this at Allied Chemical in Baton Rouge and also with the drugstores in and around the Baton Rouge area, as well as those drugstores in and around Lake Charles, Louisiana.

Ed was great at increasing union membership and quickly made Teamsters Local #5 the largest union in Baton Rouge and the surrounding areas. We eventually had seven thousand members and seven business agents. The local covered not only the capital city of Baton Rouge, but also eighteen parishes in Louisiana and three counties in the state of Mississippi.

Ed was so loved by the workers around the area that he remained boss of the local for nearly thirty years. In those early stages of my work with him, I was very proud to see how people loved and respected him. I was proud of the position he had achieved, and truly believed he was working for the good of the working man.

From My Brother's Shadow

I really believed that. I believed in Ed and in his work and was so very proud of the fact that a country boy from Wilkinson County, Mississippi, could go to a state capital and rise to such great power and notoriety, which he then was able to use to help average hard-working men and women.

And I remained very proud of Ed ... until I began realizing that things were not as they appeared.

CHAPTER 3

LIFE AS A TEAMSTER

To a great number of the Teamsters, Ed Partin was a hero. I must give him the credit he deserves: he did stand up to the big corporations. But in most things Ed was no hero. The members of Teamsters Local #5 didn't know his true motives. Like me, they thought he was standing up for working men and women, and so they let him do anything he wanted. But it wasn't that way at all. For most of his life, Ed stood up for Ed, and it brought him to a sad end.

Ed was a very smart man, and he did some good things. He helped many members of Local #5 so that they had better jobs and better lives. I personally saw and heard Teamsters tell Ed that they were about to lose their home or automobile because they had no money, and Ed, being Ed, would pull several hundred dollars out of his pocket and give it to them on the spot. To those Teamsters, Ed seemed to be a very caring and giving person. After all, he gave them money when they desperately needed it. But little did they know that what he was handing to them was bribe money. They really thought Ed was giving them money from his own pocket or paycheck.

After moving to Baton Rouge, I worked for Ed for many years, but after I began to see how things were done, I quit many times because I disagreed with his actions, and I let him know I disagreed. In the end, I always came back and worked for him again, thinking things would somehow be different. But Ed's actions and thinking never changed. If anything, they only worsened with time.

Ed controlled the majority of the construction jobs that went in and out of Baton Rouge and the surrounding areas. If a company wanted to do business in that area, Ed required that an official with that company sit down with him and make a deal before the job could begin. In this way, he became a very powerful person.

Life As a Teamster

If Ed's terms were not met, he would simply put up a picket line, and the job would come to a standstill ... until a company official agreed to meet his terms. Once Ed's terms were met by the company, the picket line would come down, work would resume, and Ed would have a few more dollars in his pocket.

Companies paid Ed for the privilege of working in the area. Not only did he receive this type of kickback; he also received, from certain companies, twenty-five cents on every cubic yard of ready-mix concrete that was hauled or poured in the surrounding area. This was a pretty lucrative affair, and it was a well known fact within the local construction industry that Ed Partin must be paid or else.

These facts were so well known that the federal government tried to catch Ed for years. They didn't succeed only because he refused to keep a bank account and, therefore, his money could never be traced.

Ed *never* used a bank. He kept his money in his attic or the walls of his house, hid it in his barn or buried it. For sure, he never left a money trail, and that made it nearly impossible for government investigators to find out where he acquired his funds.

From My Brother's Shadow

Far from being the generous person many thought he was, Ed was very possessive with his money and often downright stingy. He would have people doing all sorts of jobs for him, but he never paid them a penny of his own. Oh, he may have given a few hundred dollars here and there, to union members who were in financial trouble, to temporarily help them out, but such a "gift" was given simply to make himself look good and for no other reason.

Ed never allowed *anyone* to get involved in his personal business, especially where money was involved, and those who tried to get involved paid the price. Tommy Craig tried, and he was shot in the head and declared brain dead and died soon afterward. Jerry Sylvester tried, and he was killed in an airplane crash. Messing with Ed Partin was dangerous business — and many knew that fact.

No one ever got any money from Teamsters Local #5 or from any of Ed's "business" dealings except Ed Partin himself. It just didn't happen. If Ed found out someone had gotten so much as a dime from Teamsters funds, they would pay for the rest of their lives or pay *with* their lives!

Poor old Allen Jones (whom you will hear more about later) was accused of taking more than $20,000 from the union, but I knew Ed well enough to know that if any money left that hall, it went to Ed and no one else. I knew that for a fact. To this day, I don't know for sure the exact circumstances of how Allen Jones supposedly got his money, even though he went to jail for it. But I can tell you, with all certainty, that Ed Partin did not let anyone, other than himself, get one dime (or anything else) from the union, and he was a master at covering his trail so that few ever knew the truth.

Ed came up with some unusual means of hiding his money. Once he rented a storage unit in McComb, Mississippi, but he didn't rent it in his own name, and he was the only person who knew the name it was rented in. He needed a storage place because he often invested his cash in gold and silver coins, paintings, guns, and things of that nature that he could easily convert to cash as he needed the money. He stored many such things in that storage unit in McComb.

Later, for some reason, Ed was staying in Florida for a while, and he became ill and wasn't able to keep up with the rent payments on the storage unit. To his utter dismay, the contents of the unit were sold to pay the back rent. The person who purchased the contents of that unit received a half million dollars in gold and silver coins, guns, paintings, etc. I never knew what was paid for all those contents, but someone made the purchase of a lifetime.

As for burying money, Ed owned a home with about five acres of land in McComb. He got hold of a backhoe (I never knew if he rented it or purchased it outright), dug some deep holes around his property and buried the money in them. It was placed in large plastic containers so that it could not be located with a metal detector.

Years later, after Ed's death, Keith, one of his children, apparently attempted to find the money, but nothing was ever found (that I was aware of). I'm not sure if any of the other children tried to find it or not. Keith asked me several times if I thought his father had money hidden, and I answered as best I could at the time, but there were things I could not yet tell.

On one occasion, Ed's wife Kay discovered $35,000 hidden under the steps of their home, but that was merely pocket money for Ed. He carried that much around in a cardboard box in the trunk of his car. Aside from that stash, that's all the money that was ever found (as far as I know).

Ed sold his house and land in McComb to an attorney. I never understood exactly why he sold it.

It was a beautiful place. He had plenty of money, so I know he didn't sell it just for the money.

But even though Ed had money, he felt he couldn't let anyone know he had money. Even his wife didn't know, and when she found the thirty-five thousand under the steps, it caused some serious problems between them. Ed was very upset about that.

Ed was in prison when this happened (more on this aspect of the story later), and he called me from prison and said he needed to see me. He was so upset with Kay for finding his money that he wanted to have her killed.

Ed not only wanted Kay killed; he wanted a local business agent killed as well, because he had found out that Kay was having an affair with the man. The agent was not one of Ed's people; he was with another local union.

The fact that Kay would have an affair really hurt Ed's pride, and so he wanted me to kill them both. This was nothing new. From time to time Ed got these radical desires to have someone killed. Strangely, because he was now sitting in prison, he believed that no one could ever convict him for the murders. In his eyes, he had the perfect alibi.

From My Brother's Shadow

Thinking back on it, I suppose that Ed honestly believed I would commit murder for him. He was wrong. I arranged to meet with Kay not long afterward, and I took her to my little farm on Perrytown Road in Wilkinson County, Mississippi. After we had arrived there, I told Kay, "You know, Ed wants me to kill you."

She said, "Yes, I know."

I assured her I was not going to do it, and we talked at length about the entire situation. I guess Kay thought enough of me to know I wouldn't have done such a thing.

One of the reasons Ed never confided in anyone, when it came to money, was that he didn't want anyone to be able to testify against him in a court of law. But Mother also discovered some of Ed's hidden money on two different occasions. She often stayed with Ed, doing baby-sitting, cleaning the house, cooking or doing whatever else he needed her to do at the time. Ed was still her boy.

On one occasion, when Ed was living in Prairieville, Louisiana, Mother kept noticing that he was making frequent trips to the attic. One day, when Ed was not home, she decided to go up there and see what in the world he was doing up there. After nosing around a little, she found what she later described to me as a space between the 2 X 6 rafters filled with new twenty-dollar bills still in their wrappers.

Another time, Ed had bought a home in the Shenandoah Subdivision in Baton Rouge, and Mother was staying with him again. One day she noticed a lot of cardboard boxes in his closet. She later told me she looked in those boxes and found that they, too, were full of new twenty-dollar bills still in the wrappers. I asked her if she took any of that money, and she said, "No, son, but I sure wanted to."

Ed's salary from Teamsters Local #5 was whatever he wanted it to be, because he was the boss, and the unions were still strong at the time. Those seven thousand union members each paid $20 to $30 a month in union dues.

The dues varied. For example, if a worker was paid $10 an hour, he would pay $20 a month in union dues, as they were calculated at two times a worker's hourly wage. So seven thousand union members paying a minimum of $20 would total $140,000 a month.

That was a great deal of money, then and now, but that was not the total income of the local. Fifteen hundred of those union members worked on construction jobs, and money was "collected," so to speak, for Ed at the various job sites. If someone wanted to work on a particular construction site, he had to pay Ed $20 to $25 a week for the privilege. This money was collected by union stewards, and it was in addition to the monthly dues.

Union stewards were handpicked by Ed. If a person held that title, he was allowed, by union rules, to go onto a job site and talk to the union workers. It was then that they collected this money.

After collecting the money from the workers on the job sites, the union stewards would take the money back to the union hall and turn it over to the business agents, who would count it. I was told that there were times when an employee's check would be taken and cashed, and the required monies were deducted by the union stewards before the balance of the employee's pay was taken back to him on the job site.

I never saw it happen, but I always believed that this money was then given to Ed, and if any worker failed to pay Ed's $20, he was issued a layoff slip. According to my calculations, that would have amounted to some $30,000 a week. That's why Ed was always rolling in money.

The $20 to $25 a week collected on the job sites was from construction workers only, and they had no choice but to pay in order to keep their jobs.

Life As a Teamster

They were depending on Teamsters Union Local #5 to keep them in work. This money was sometimes referred to as "Ed's legal money," in other words, money to pay attorneys' fees.

I contributed to that fund twice, but when I realized there would be no end to the collecting, I quit paying and, because I was the boss' brother, I got away with it. When my unhappiness with this system became apparent, Ed made sure that no one ever spoke to me again about these monies. It was still collected, but no one mentioned it.

By doing a little math, I came to the conclusion that Ed had a fund of some $260,000 a month, more than a quarter of a million dollars, that he could draw from, and that didn't include the kickbacks he was paid directly. Yes, Ed had money, so much of it he had to find places to hide it and bury it. Over a twelve month period, Ed could have easily hidden away millions of dollars.

As a child, I had grown up in the shadow of this older brother, watching and learning from him as I grew, and as I grew into manhood, I continued watching and learning. Now, in this new environment, as I worked alongside Ed (still in his shadow), I found myself disagreeing with much of what he did and how he did it, and I resented being used by him in this way.

How was I personally being used by Ed? In so many ways. For instance, because I had more education than Ed, there were things I could do better than he, for example letter writing, and he was ever ready to capitalize on my talents. When Ed needed to write a letter, he called on me to write it for him. He would tell me whom to write to and the general gist of what he wanted said, but then he depended on me to actually word the letter. When it was written, he would usually change something, even if it was just a single word, so that no one else could receive the credit for having written it. He had made it his own. It was now Ed's letter, and I was left in his shadow once again.

But I can tell you one thing: in his shadow or not, I was learning. I was learning the ropes of Local #5 in Baton Rouge. I was learning the correct way to do things and watching the way my brother did things. At the time, I had no idea that I was grooming myself to actually replace him. I had no idea what the future held; I was working *with* Ed.

I worked outside the union hall on jobs, but I also spent many hours at the hall itself, seeing and hearing things on a daily basis. I saw some good things and some not-so-good things, and I began to wonder about how a great number of things were handled and how Ed was able to pull off a lot of the things he seemed to get away with. In my own mind, I began to question some of his actions and his dealings, for I was seeing and hearing many things I could not agree with.

This all took place in the mid 1950s and early 1960s. It was during those years that I, verbally and through my actions, disagreed with Ed, and I quit my position many times because of it.

Many poor Teamsters were sitting around the union hall depending on Ed to find them a job. All one could hear around the hall was "Yes, Boss," "Okay, Boss," and "What can I do for you, Boss?" The Teamsters would do anything the boss wanted. Ed liked that, being called Boss, and conversely, no one ever bossed Ed. If anyone tried it, they had to go. That was Ed's way.

The Teamsters literally had to kiss Ed's ass in order to work. That's what it amounted to. Those whom Ed had working were poor men who could not find a good paying job anywhere else. Some of them were from Mississippi and had worked a while as loggers or at some other arduous and challenging task. They came to Ed, and he gave them jobs making $15 to $20 an hour, and that was really good money back then. They worked on pipeline construction or movie jobs that would last six to eight months, and they could take home $1,500 or more per week. Teamsters members wanted those jobs, and so they did whatever they needed to do in order to get them and keep them.

Ed had no organized method of fairly assigning those jobs, and therefore the "best ass kissers" were assigned the best jobs. It took me a while, but I finally realized what was actually going on and what Ed was doing. I know what I'm talking about because I was there, and I witnessed it personally.

I was in my late twenties when one day I accompanied Ed to the Bellemont Hotel in Baton Rouge. He and I entered the restaurant, but he told me to sit at a certain table and wait for him, and then he went to sit at another table. Before long, a man entered and sat down at the table with Ed. I recognized the man immediately as the owner of a ready-mix concrete company. In due course, I saw the man slip Ed an envelope under the table.

After I thought about it a while, I realized that our local had never given this particular man and his company any trouble, while we were continually causing trouble for similar companies. It was in that moment that I realized just what was really going on.

That whole scene was very hurtful to me. It was something I had never wanted to see my older brother doing, and it was difficult for me to face the reality of it all.

I never said a word to Ed about that incident, but from that moment on I began watching things much more closely. I saw companies being shut down, equipment being sabotaged, deals being made, by Ed, for certain companies to supply free materials for the home he was building, petitions being withdrawn for membership into the Teamsters and so many other wrong things.

On one occasion, Ed called me and asked me to intervene in the River Bend Nuclear Power Plant construction job. He had learned that the truck drivers hauling sand and gravel to the site were non-union drivers, and he told me I had to find a way to shut their trucks down. I did what Ed instructed me to do, and the job was shut down.

The very next day an official with the sand and gravel company in question approached me and said for me to tell Ed there was no way he could conceal such a large sum of up-front money. I had no idea what he was talking about, but I told him that I would tell Ed. I never did. People often came to me and told me to relay some message to Ed, I guess because I was his brother, and they assumed I was well informed about everything Ed did.

Shortly after that, a man by the name of Bill Tygress looked me up and came to see me. Bill was known as the "fixer" in the St. Francisville, Louisiana area. He told me he had made a deal with the sand and gravel company to pay Ed five cents for every yard of sand and gravel delivered to the River Bend Nuclear Power Plant job site.

Both of those men, the official from the sand and gravel company and Bill Tygress, thought that because I was Ed's brother I must be involved in any deals Ed made. But the truth is that I wasn't involved in any of this. I was simply doing what I was told to do by Ed. He was my big brother, but he was also my boss.

Several days later Ed called me again. This time he instructed me to go to a small airport in St. Francisville and pick up a suitcase from an incoming flight. I went to the airport, as he had instructed, and after waiting for a while, I saw a plane coming in for a landing. When it had taxied to a stop, a man stepped off the plane and asked me if I were Doug Partin. I told him, "Yes." He then returned to the plane and came back carrying a suitcase. He handed me the suitcase and a key and then turned around, without another word, boarded the plane and left.

Ed had instructed me not to look in the suitcase but to bring it to him immediately. I was, of course, curious and so I looked in the suitcase. What I saw were wrapped twenty-dollar bills. The suitcase was packed to the limit with them. I estimated the contents to be approximately $300,000.

I was nervous when I met Ed in the parking lot of the Ramada Inn Hotel on Airline Highway in Baton Rouge that day and handed him the suitcase and key. I never confessed to him that I had looked inside and knew what it contained. I didn't want to be involved with Ed's doings in any other way. All I wanted was a legal job, to earn a legal salary and support my family.

As he took the suitcase, Ed instructed me to return to St. Francisville, to the River Bend Nuclear Power Plant job site, and to allow the trucks to go back to work, hauling sand and gravel for the job. He left with the suitcase and key, which I never saw again (and never wanted to see again). So, you see, I know what I'm talking about. It happened.

When we would go out on strike, out on a picket line, and people on that picket line were beaten up, we, as Ed's workers, were beaten up, too. That was a totally different thing. But to see Ed get paid to take a picket line down or paid kickbacks for any reason, while Teamsters were on that line fighting for work, was totally against everything I believed in and still believe in to this day. It was all just so wrong.

I remember seeing ex-football players from Louisiana State University in Baton Rouge being given jobs by Ed. He sent some of those non-dues paying football players out on good jobs while dues-paying Teamsters members of twenty years or more sat there in the meeting hall, out of work, waiting and hoping for any job.

Ed also gave several of the football players the position of business agent, and that really hurt me. By now I was a business agent myself, but I had worked hard for it. These men just had it given to them. But Ed was the boss, and so I said nothing. Ed paid those football players he hired a larger salary than he was paying me for the same position. That, too, hurt me, and Ed knew it.

Ed never seemed to want me to have any kind of authority in the union. As usual, he wanted total control over me and everyone else around him. If I had kowtowed to his every desire, maybe it would have been different. I couldn't do that.

Life As a Teamster

Ed was a big sports fan and especially of the Louisiana State University football team. He bragged to me that he could have been an LSU football player and said he had once tried out for the team. But Ed had a problem with following rules; he would not live by anyone's rules except his own, so playing football for LSU didn't work out, or so he said.

Ed hired those football players, and many of them went everywhere he went, for he used them as bodyguards. Billy Cannon and Jimmy Taylor were two of the players Ed hired, and they often traveled with him. Of course, Billy Cannon was a Heisman Trophy winner, and having Billy hanging around him made Ed feel big and proud.

Let me say here that Billy Cannon is one of the finest people I have ever known. He has had some legal problems through the years, but that has not hindered my appreciation for him as a person.

Whether it was Billy or Jimmy or someone else, everywhere Ed went someone was tagging along with him. Some of these were considered to be his "bodyguards," and bodyguards were never allowed to sit at the same table with him when they were out in a public place. The bodyguards sat at a different table, and just watched for Ed's safety.

From My Brother's Shadow

Every time I had a disagreement with Ed, I struggled with what to do. He was my brother, and I didn't want to hurt him in any way, but I really had no choice. I had to do what was right and fair, whether Ed liked it or not. And often he didn't.

As I've noted before, Ed was a very smart man in his own way and very good at what he did, and I appreciated everything he did for me and others. He was probably the best union leader Local #5 ever had or maybe ever will have, but the way he conducted business left a lot to be desired. I was told by Ossie Brown, a District Attorney in Baton Rouge, that if Ed had received a college education he would probably have become governor of Louisiana. I think Ossie was right.

Ed was usually a very nice looking man, but in time his appearance started to go downhill. He began wearing soiled clothes, and he constantly chain smoked. There were serious nicotine stains on his fingers and even on his pockets where he put his hands.

He became very agitated and started taking a lot of prescription pills. He had to take pills to get himself going in the morning and pills to help him relax and sleep at night. Once, when we were in negotiations over a contract, I saw Ed take enough pills to help keep him awake all night. He never blinked an eye the whole night long. Everyone else attending the meeting found a place to get some sleep, and the snoring was so loud it was unreal. I eventually found a spot on a sofa myself and went to sleep, but Ed was still going strong.

I hated to see Ed taking all those pills, but that was Ed, and he did whatever the hell he wanted to do. I could never manage to discuss the problem with him. Believe me, I tried. He wouldn't listen. As far as Ed was concerned, he had no problem, but Ed's problems were just beginning.

CHAPTER 4

THE TYRANNICAL 60s

During the late 1950s and on into the 1960s I continued to work in the shadow of my brother, and during that time, I saw so much and heard so much that it was almost unbearable at times. The union membership was constantly growing and, as it grew, so did the hectic, eventful, and often dangerous activities surrounding Teamsters Local #5, its members and its officers.

Suspicious union activities, allegations against union members and officers, and legal charges and indictments against union members and officers began to appear in the local newspapers almost daily. And, take my word for it, many of them were well founded. I was there, and I heard and witnessed much of it. To some extent, I was involved in many of the things that were taking place at the time, so I know.

I avoided the illegal and questionable activities, and the things I involved myself with were legitimate and needful for everyone's benefit. I honestly thought at the time that I was doing the right thing for everyone involved. I was learning the correct way to handle things, even as I saw them being done in an incorrect way. Unbeknownst to me at the time, I was being groomed for the future.

As I said before, many times I got disgusted with Ed and the way he was conducting union activities and quit. In the end, however, I would always tell him that because he was my brother, I would do anything for him, except go to prison. So I refused to force any person to pay a bribe; I refused to have anyone beaten up; and I refused to make a deal with any company that involved a payoff. I simply would not do those things.

On one particular occasion, when I had quit working for Ed, a friend and I went into business together. It was a small trucking business. Ed had our trucks sabotaged. Because I knew he would continue those same tactics until we had been bankrupted, I sold my share of the business to my partner, so that he would be able to make a living without the constant fear of Ed trying to ruin his business.

For his part, Ed wanted me around and available to help him when he needed me, and, for my part, I had a family of four children and a wife to support, and so I needed a job. Each time I quit working for Ed he would somehow get word to me that he needed me — when he found himself in trouble, or when he was required to go to trial in places like Atlanta, or Butte, Montana, or Houston, or San Diego, or Baton Rouge or Shreveport, Louisiana, just to name a few. Every time he had to go somewhere else for trial, or wanted to take a vacation or get away for any reason, he wanted me there to oversee things at the Teamsters hall until he could get back. And I did that for him each time he asked me to, just trying to help him out.

With me there, Ed knew he wouldn't have to worry about someone trying to take over the local or turn evidence on him, or anything like that. He trusted me to take care of things in his absence, and I didn't let him down. That was the ten percent of me that Ed wanted alive to help him out when he needed me. I'll tell you about the remaining ninety percent later. Ed and I had what some might call a love/hate relationship. In some ways, he may have hated me, but he knew that I would do what was right and take care of Local #5 whenever he asked me to.

Officially, my position with the local was Business Agent and Trustee. I even ran for the office of president on one occasion. As noted earlier, this position is secondary in a local, but it is next in line to the principal officer. Even though Ed would call me in to work at the union hall in his absence, acting on his behalf, or in his capacity, so to speak, he didn't want me to hold the position of president. He didn't want me to have any real power or be in any position to have a say-so about what was right or what was wrong in the union, because he knew that I would not do anything wrong or take a chance on going to prison. He was also afraid I would try to take his job. I would never have done that, but that was the way Ed thought. I suppose his mistrust stemmed from the way he himself got the job in the first place.

When I decided to run for president of the local, Ed proceeded to call in all of his union stewards from their jobs for a meeting at the hall. Unfortunately, I walked in on them unknowingly as they were conducting the meeting. I knew instantly exactly what the meeting was about, so I told them, "Well, boys, you beat me." They said the election had not yet been held. I said, "Yes, it has. It's been held right here today. I know I'm going to lose this election, but I'm telling all of you this: I will be back." And, with that, I turned and walked out of the meeting.

As I had predicted, I lost the election. Ed had given each of the job stewards who had gathered that day the title of business agent and instructed them to go back to their individual job sites and tell the union members to vote against me. As business agents, they had authority, according to union by-laws, to go on the job sites and talk to all the union members.

Even though I lost the election for president, I did continue as assistant business agent. Strangely, after I had lost that election for president, Ed arranged for me to be appointed to the executive board of the local. I guess he did that thinking it would satisfy me.

But Ed could really do some strange things, and it really didn't matter much to me at the time. All I wanted to do was what was right for the members. I didn't like what was going on in the union, and

Ed knew that. He tried every way in the world he could to make me understand what he was trying to do, but all I could see was that Ed was using the union members for his own ends. The more I learned about the local and about how it worked and the more I saw of how Ed operated, the more I understood that things were not being done correctly, and it really hurt me. I had clung to the idealistic thought that the union was doing everything it could to help poor working men and women, but I was learning that this was not always the case.

As for Ed, he continued to use me, as he did others. At one point, he filed for personal bankruptcy. I never knew why. I suppose that, for some reason, he could not get his hands on his well-hidden stashes of money, for fear of raising questions about how he had obtained them. Whatever the reason, when he needed a new car, he couldn't buy one in his own name. He came to me and asked me to buy a car for him in *my* name. He would make the payments somehow through the local. I did as Ed asked, but not many months had gone by before a man showed up at my house one day asking why the notes on the car were not being paid. I had thought Ed was paying, so this came as a total shock to me. The man wanted all the past-due money owed on the car, or he wanted the car. Ed had the car at the Teamsters hall, so I picked up the phone and called him right then. I asked if he had been paying the notes on the car, and he said, "Yes."

The man who had come to collect the past-due amount or take the car got on the phone to his office and complained that we were saying the notes had been paid. The office staff checked again and assured him that they had not. Ed was so insistent that I felt I had to take his part, and one thing led to another, until the collection agent and I got into a very heated argument, and I physically threw him out of my house. He was so frightened that he ran right past his parked car and kept on running, although he had lost one of his shoes. Someone came and took the car away, but the man never did come back for the shoe.

Furious, I went right to the union hall to confront Ed about the whole situation. When I asked him if he was sure he had paid the notes on the car, he started laughing at me, and he just sat there and laughed. I had just gotten into a physical altercation with a collection agent over this mess, and all Ed could do was laugh about it.

From My Brother's Shadow

As it turned out, Ed had been lying to me all along. He had not paid the notes on the car, and that should not have surprised me. He had not paid a single note. The car was soon paid for though. Somehow it caught fire right there in front of the union hall. It was a total loss, and the insurance company paid it off.

I never knew why Ed had not paid the notes or why he had found it necessary to lie to me about it. It would not have been anything for him to have the local pay. But that was Ed. You never knew why he was doing something. Well, now he was on foot again and, as far as I was concerned, he could get another car the best way he could. He should not count on my help.

Ed used those he called friends in many ways. For example, he had a close friend by the name of Emmett Tucker. Emmett would do just about anything for Ed. No, I must correct myself. Emmett would do *anything* for Ed.

At one point, Teamsters Local #5 was expelled from the international organization for its failure to pay the required per capita taxes. However, sometime after the trial and imprisonment of Jimmy Hoffa, the organization agreed to accept Local #5 back into fellowship, if a payment of

$25,000 in back per capita taxes were made. To pay the required $25,000 Ed decided to persuade several Teamsters from the local to borrow money for him in their own names. I didn't know about any of this until it was a done deal. Emmett Tucker was put in charge of lining up members who would sign notes with the bank in the amount of $5,000 each. He ran into a little trouble finding enough willing members. One man initially agreed, but then his wife approached Emmett and asked him to let her husband off the hook because they couldn't afford it. Her pleading was unfruitful because Emmett was just following Ed's instructions.

After Emmett had persuaded five Teamsters to sign a note for $5,000 each, they all met one night at a certain banker's home to work out the loan details. How the banker was able to get all that approved at the bank I have no idea. But the Teamsters received the loan proceeds, and they brought the money directly to Ed. The back per capita taxes were paid, and the local was reinstated, but sadly, the men who signed the promissory notes with Ed's assurance of repayment never saw a dime of those funds returned.

That was the Ed Partin I knew, and that was the way he conducted business. I don't understand why he did those Teamsters the way he did, and, again, I knew nothing about the arrangement until later. I would not have agreed to the deal, and I certainly would not have signed one of those notes. That's the reason I was not asked to participate and why I was not even told about the plan or how it evolved.

Because I learned the hard way how Ed operated, if I had known about that scheme, I certainly would have warned those Teamsters that they would never get their money back and would have tried my damnedest to talk them out of signing those notes.

The time was now nearing for union elections, and Ed began getting a little nervous and anxious. He didn't want anyone running against him in the upcoming election. When a person was on what was called "withdrawal," according to union rules, he could not run for office for the next three years. Union members were required to have paid union dues for three years straight without being on withdrawal to be eligible to run for office in the union. There were thirteen people Ed feared might run against him in the upcoming election. So he took money from the union and, with it, bought thirteen withdrawal cards, effectively making those thirteen individuals ineligible to run against him. This transaction did not involve a large sum of money, but eventually Ed was charged with thirteen counts of embezzlement, for having taken union money to pay for the withdrawal cards. He was also charged with thirteen counts of falsifying records, which involved the actual creation of the withdrawal cards. That was Ed Partin. He was something. He was *really* something.

Another of the many charges filed against Ed through the years involved a fatal automobile accident in Alabama. He was indicted in 1962 for manslaughter and for leaving the scene of an accident. According to him, he blacked out and could not remember what actually happened to cause the accident. The truth is that he knew exactly what had happened.

There was a soldier involved in the accident, and that soldier's blood was all over Ed's car, a brand-new 1962 Oldsmobile Ninety-Eight. Ed sent a Teamster to quickly take the car to Mexico, where we had friends. Unfortunately that Teamster was stopped by officials in Mexico as he was driving around town in the car with no registration papers. He was arrested and taken to jail. He somehow got word to Ed in Baton Rouge that he was in jail in Mexico and asked Ed to get him out. Ed sent Emmett Tucker and me to Mexico to try to get the man released.

Once we had processed the needed papers, I went to the jail to get the Teamster out, but he refused to go with me, fearing that I, the boss' brother, was going to kill him. I left and sent Emmett back to get the man out, and he willingly left with Emmett.

The car had originally been impounded in Old Laredo, Mexico, but the FBI had already gotten it moved to Laredo, Texas, and now it was impounded there. When Ed heard about it, he sent some Teamsters to Laredo and had them steal the car from the police impound lot, but the FBI had already gotten scrapings from the car. Ed immediately had some body work done on the vehicle, but it was too late. The scrapings the FBI had gotten matched the scrapings found on the body of the dead soldier.

So Ed had lied again. He was so good at it that he could fool any lie detector test he was given. (I'll get a little deeper into that subject later.)

In those critical 1960s, things were heating up at the union hall, and they were heating up on the individual job sites.

The Tyrannical 60s

The Louisiana Creamery strike began in January of 1963, and that strike lasted for several years. It was very violent, and a lot of people were physically injured in the process. Dynamite was employed, and some very tough fights took place.

Louisiana Creamery was the largest milk producer in the Baton Rouge area, and the Teamsters voted to strike it because the milk deliverymen and some of the production employees had come to the Teamsters hall asking to be unionized and reporting that they were being abused in the workplace. The creamery officials declined to meet with union officials to discuss unionization of their employees, so we put those workers on strike.

During this strike, some of our Teamsters were indicted on various charges, and I actually had guns pulled on and pointed at me personally. It was a very big mess.

The first time dynamite was used at the creamery, the fuses fizzled out, but some months later there was a huge explosion there. A lot of dynamite was being used around the Baton Rouge area at the time, and things were being blown up. I say *things*, because I never knew what things. I didn't ask. I do know the dynamite was being purchased in Mexico.

From My Brother's Shadow

At one point, as things continued to heat up, the dynamite needed to be disposed of before it was discovered by authorities. Three Teamsters loaded it all into a U-Haul trailer and took it to the Homochitto National Forest in Mississippi.

Once inside the national forest, they attached a long fuse to the trailer full of dynamite and ran like hell. The sky lit up for miles around, and windows were blown out of nearby houses. A local newspaper ran an interesting article on the mysterious explosion the next day. Evidently a meteorite had hit the Homochitto National Forest, and there were actually a couple of eye-witnesses to the strange event.

Because Creamery officials insisted on hiring non-union deliverymen, their delivery trucks were now being followed and harassed, which led to some fist fights and brawls. Many men were beaten up, and Ed, as leader of the Teamsters local at the time, was charged as being responsible for those violent acts. I honestly don't think Ed was guilty of actually participating in any of those fights. He may have known about them, but he was smart enough to know to stay out of any actual physical altercation. He always had someone else do his physical work for him.

The Tyrannical 60s

The job of organizing the maintenance employees of the East Baton Rouge Parish School Board was one job I will never forget, and it was the angriest I ever got with my brother. I had no idea he was going to sell the school maintenance employees out. We had the school system beat. By "we," I mean the business agents of Teamsters Local #5. We had worked hard to organize those maintenance employees, and we had them signed up to become Teamsters. The teachers were on strike, and the Teamsters were on strike, and the garbage was piling up at the schools because the city garbage workers were Teamsters, and they refused to cross the picket lines at the schools. This put the East Baton Rouge School System in a serious bind. They were going to *have* to sign a contract with the Teamsters; they really had no choice.

Because of all this, I couldn't understand why Ed did what he did next. He set up a big meeting of all the East Baton Rouge Parish School System employees at the Baton Rouge Centroplex and, once everyone was gathered, he stepped up to the microphone and announced that the Teamsters were withdrawing from the whole affair. He had thought it over the night before, he said, and he felt in his heart that it would not be right for the

From My Brother's Shadow

Teamsters to organize the employees of the school board. This was *not* a Teamsters decision. It was something that Ed Partin decided on his own. Why? No one knew.

Several other business agents and I had worked very hard over the past months, signing up twelve hundred new Teamsters members from among the school board employees (while Ed was off vacationing or hiding somewhere), and now, with one stroke, he had annulled all of our hard work. It was painful, but what could I do? Ed was the Boss, and that's just the way it was. I really didn't understand why he felt he had to sell us out as he did.

But the whole thing just didn't make sense. Twelve hundred new union members would have meant more union dues for Local #5 and better working conditions and pay for the school board employees. Somehow and for some reason, Ed suddenly wasn't concerned about new members, about more money coming in or about how his little brother felt about it all. He just wanted to look like a big man, and so he reveled in his speech about not allowing the Teamsters to come in and unionize the school system.

In a similar way, I also worked on organizing the workers of a company in nearby Denham Springs,

Louisiana. I had already managed to sign up more than a hundred people to become new members of Teamsters Local #5, when I received a phone call one day from Ed. He asked me to meet him at the Pancake House on Airline Highway in Baton Rouge and told me he had someone he wanted me to meet. When I arrived at the restaurant, Ed introduced me to the man, and I recognized him as the owner of the company I was even then organizing. Ed informed me that the man was going to furnish some of the building materials for a house he wanted to build in McComb, and because of it, he had turned over to him all of the applications of those I had managed to sign up so far.

Wow! Now the owner of the company knew exactly which of his employees had signed up to unionize the plant, and he probably went back and fired every single one of them. Again, Ed had sold me out, along with all of those employees, so that he could get some building materials for the home he was building.

When Ed instructed me to withdraw the petition with the National Labor Relations Board regarding those employees, I refused. At that point, he really became mad and let me know, in no uncertain terms, that he was Secretary-Treasurer/Business

From My Brother's Shadow

Manager of the Teamsters Local #5 and that he would withdraw the petition himself. I told him if he did I would quit. True to his word, Ed withdrew the petition, and, true to my word, I quit ... again.

I went to the union hall, got a referral slip, and put myself on a construction job driving a truck. Ed found out which job I was working on and sent word by different Teamsters that he wanted me to come back. This went on for a month or two ... until Ed had to go out of state to appear in court. As usual, he needed me, and, as usual, I gave in and went back to the hall and took his place while he was away.

Some of the things Ed did were so strange that only he could possibly have understood why he did them. One of those strange things he did was to start the Independent Local 100 in Baton Rouge. Much later, I came to realize why he did it.

I had worked very hard on that job, too, organizing the Department of Public Works employees of the City of Baton Rouge. It was a huge challenge. I had told Ed that we could organize them, but he was very skeptical. I insisted that we could do it, so he told me to go ahead and try. He placed me and several other business agents in charge of this project, and we went to work.

The Tyrannical 60s

The phone began ringing at the union hall, and people were calling asking Ed if he was trying to organize the Department of Public Works. He told all those callers that he didn't know anything about it, that *I* was the one trying to organize them.

Ed then left town and went to a home he had in Flagstaff, Arizona, and remained there for a while. In fact, he remained there until he was sure we had the Department of Public Works employees signed up and ready to vote to join the Teamsters. Only then did he return to Baton Rouge.

As we were in the process of signing up all those public works employees, I had assured them that they would be accepted as Teamsters and this would give them a voice in the local and also in the International Brotherhood of Teamsters Union. But, for some strange reason, when Ed got back to Baton Rouge, he started another union called Public Employees Union Local 100. It wasn't affiliated with the Teamsters, or any other union. In the process, he made it appear as though *I* had misled all those public works employees. Ed's time in Flagstaff had evidently been well spent planning this next scheme. I had organized the City of Baton Rouge and, in the process, gotten three thousand new members for Teamsters Local #5, and now

From My Brother's Shadow

Ed had started the Local 100 and undone all that I had achieved.

Ed assigned his buddy, Billy Cannon, as President of Local 100, even though Billy had never worked in a union before and didn't know anything about running a union. Talk about being pissed! I was pissed off!

Billy later asked me to help him out with the union, but I told him, "No," that he was on his own. Ed didn't like that and told me I was to help Billy. I told him that Billy was the damn President of that organization and that he should know what he was doing, so let him do it. And I refused to help Billy. It was with Local 100 that Ed eventually got caught taking money and was sent to prison as a result. I'll get into the details of all that later.

Local 100 was a public employees' union, and as such, it was not required to file all the paperwork with the National Labor Relations Board and the Department of Labor that other types of unions were required to file. Because the members were public employees, the union was exempted. I'm convinced that this was the reason Ed decided to develop an independent union (that he named Local 100). Also, more importantly to Ed, he could control such a union.

Think about that. There were three thousand members in the new union, each one paying dues, and they didn't have to give a cut to any national organization. Ed was a smart man, wasn't he?

This reminded me of the statement made by District Attorney Ossie Brown: "If Ed had gone to college, he would have become the governor of Louisiana." Yes, I believe Ed could have pulled that off, too.

CHAPTER 5

LEGAL CHARGES AND INDICTMENTS

Even though Ed's criminal record was widely reported to have begun in 1959, when he was charged with assault in St. Helena Parish, Louisiana, by a contractor, it actually began back in his teenage years with the theft of all those guns from the hardware store in Natchez, Mississippi. Then, during the 1960s, Ed was indicted on many charges. They ranged from forgery, perjury and manslaughter, to kidnapping. But, he was never convicted of any of these charges.

From My Brother's Shadow

For some reason, the assault charges against him in St. Helena Parish were later withdrawn. Think about that.

In 1962 Ed was indicted in that automobile accident in Alabama for manslaughter and leaving the scene of a fatal accident. He was never convicted. Think about that.

In January of 1962 Ed was indicted by the East Baton Rouge Grand Jury for forgery. Six months later he was charged by a Federal Grand Jury in New Orleans on thirteen counts of falsification of records and thirteen counts of embezzlement.

In September of 1962 Ed and three other individuals were indicted for aggravated kidnapping.

In October of 1962 the Federal forgery and embezzlement charges that were pending against Ed were suddenly continued to a future date. That happened to be the same month Jimmy Hoffa's trial began in Nashville.

The aggravated kidnapping charges were very serious, Ed knew it, and it really shook him up. If he were to be convicted on such serious charges, they would carry very stiff sentences and he dreaded that prospect.

I was with Ed the day he was informed that he had been indicted on federal kidnapping charges. He and a close friend and associate named Billy Simpson were visiting me at my home, and the three of us were standing outside near Ed's car when a telephone I had in the garage rang. I went to answer it, and someone asked for Billy, so I called him to the phone. Billy talked on the phone for a minute or so, and then he came back out to the car where Ed and I were. By this time, Ed had gotten into the car and was sitting there waiting on Billy.

Billy had a strange look on his face, and he told Ed, "I've just been indicted."

"For what?" Ed asked.

"For kidnapping," Billy answered.

This caused Ed to laugh, and he said to Billy, "What in the world are you talking about?"

But Billy wasn't laughing.

Ed asked Billy, "How did you get involved in kidnapping?"

Billy said, "Look, Ed, they got you too. They got you for kidnapping."

Hearing this, Ed was visibly shaken.

Ed asked me if he could make a phone call from my home. I always believed it was to Jimmy Hoffa. I was told later that Ed had tried to call Hoffa several times, after he found out he was facing the kidnapping charges and that Hoffa had also called the local Teamsters hall several times looking for Ed. That day Ed decided to leave his car parked at my home and had me take him, in my car, all the way to Shreveport, Louisiana, a two-hundred-and-fifty-mile drive to the northwest. All during that trip, Ed was lying under a blanket on the backseat of my car, hoping no one would discover him.

When we arrived in Shreveport, I purchased Ed an airplane ticket to Washington, DC. He was determined to go there to see Jimmy Hoffa personally, hoping that Hoffa could somehow get him out of this trouble.

After Ed had left, I drove back home. Ed had asked me to drive around Baton Rouge a little in the car he left at my house, in the hope that it would be spotted, and the local authorities would think he was still in town. I made just one trip in that car, as I remember it, to a little drive-in restaurant not far from my house, to get a burger. On the way back home, I suddenly found myself surrounded by all sorts of police vehicles. Officers quickly placed me in handcuffs, later telling me they had thought I was Ed. When they realized I wasn't Ed, they tried to think of something they could arrest me for. After quite some time, they weren't able to come up with anything.

Legal Charges and Indictments

Eventually they asked if I had a pink slip or registration for the car. I said I didn't. They kept the handcuffs on me but now took me to my home.

When we arrived at my home, the police told me they would remove the handcuffs and drop all charges if I would agree to sign an authorization for them to search my home without a warrant. I agreed, and they proceeded to do the search.

They not only searched through the house; they went under the house and up into the attic, searching any and every possible hiding place. During this whole time, my wife and children were hiding under a bed, terrorized. I knew my wife had a gun, and I was afraid she would panic and shoot one of the officers doing the search. Fortunately we all made it through that ordeal without anyone being hurt.

I was released, but the authorities impounded Ed's car, and, I'm sure, thoroughly searched it. As it turned out, the pink slip or registration had been in the car all along.

When those kidnapping charges against Ed and Billy Simpson surfaced, there were many other charges still pending against Ed. These particular charges involved the disappearance of Billy's two children. They were two years old, and ten months old respectively, and Billy's estranged wife had been awarded legal custody of them by the court. But Billy had refused to reveal their location either to his estranged wife or to the authorities and, as result, he was arrested and put in jail on contempt of court charges.

Besides Billy and Ed, two other people were indicted on the kidnapping charges: Jackie Simpson, and Mrs. Healon Simpson, both close relatives of Billy. According to reports issued on September 9, 1962, they, too, were being sought by the authorities.

Billy Simpson was already in trouble. He and five other Teamsters were facing disturbing the peace charges, in regard to a fight which took place at the union hall on April 11, 1962. Two former Teamsters were allegedly beaten that day. As a matter of fact, my other brother, Donald, was one of the six members indicted on those charges.

Billy Simpson's wife was called to testify at the trial against these six Teamsters. As of September 14, 1962, Mrs. Simpson still did not know the whereabouts of her two small children. She stated that she was told that her children would be hidden where they would never be found, and that if she ever wanted to see them again, it would be best for her to forget about testifying against the

Legal Charges and Indictments

Teamsters. Meanwhile, the three other people facing the kidnapping charges were still at large. In my estimation, this whole kidnapping incident was nothing more than a ploy of sorts to keep Mrs. Simpson from testifying against the Teamsters.

At this point, I must stop to share a little of the history between Ed Partin and Billy Simpson. Billy was considered a tough guy, and that reputation was probably the number one reason Ed allowed Billy to hang around. In 1962, Billy was about twenty and Ed was about thirty-nine. It was strongly rumored that Ed was having an affair with Billy's wife.

I received a phone call from Ed one day, asking me to come and get him at a private residence (not his own). When I arrived at the place, I saw that Ed had been cut badly on his back and was bleeding profusely. I took him to a doctor, and he was stitched up. According to Ed, Billy Simpson had cut him with a knife.

This is all background for the kidnapping charges that resulted against Billy, Ed and the others. Ed had nothing to do with the actual kidnapping of those children, at least not the physical act itself. For all I know, it could have been a well-planned plot between Billy and Ed. But the truth of the matter is that Ed had loaned or given Billy Simpson his car and some money in order to get him out of town with his children after Billy's wife had been awarded legal custody. Billy took the children to New Orleans and left them in the care of his aunt, who lived there. I know this for a fact because I was involved in a round-about way, having later been called upon to take money to the aunt for the care of the children. Ed handed me the money one day and told me where to take it, and that's all I knew. I was just following his instructions, but if I had been caught, I, too, would probably have been charged with kidnapping.

It didn't end there. I was not alone in that money run. There were three of us who made that trip to New Orleans — Emmett Tucker, my brother Donald and myself. The trip was more than a little nerve racking because we had FBI agents following us, and we knew it. So we had to shake them off. We went through hell and back, and all because Ed had asked us to do him a favor.

In time Ed found himself sitting behind bars in a Baton Rouge jail on those kidnapping charges. What an irony that was! When I think back on all of Ed's other questionable activities and his devious schemes, I have to marvel at what it was that finally got him.

Legal Charges and Indictments

Meanwhile, newspapers and television stations nationwide were reporting on the troubles Teamsters boss Jimmy Hoffa was then facing himself. He was under a serious indictment stemming from his involvement in an alleged criminal deal with a certain trucking firm. The company in question was alleged to have paid him $242,000 in bribes. The case was very well publicized, and many are familiar with the facts of the case — especially Teamsters from that period.

At the same time, Ed was now sitting behind bars on the kidnapping charges. He had gotten himself into a real predicament, and he knew it. This imprisonment was particularly trying for him because, although he never spoke about it, rumor had it that Ed had grown accustomed to taking certain drugs, and now he couldn't get his hands on them.

It should be noted, also, that when Ed turned himself in on those kidnapping charges, serious steps were taken to make sure he wasn't caught with any drugs in his possession. We bought him a new suit of clothes and had all of the pockets sewn shut. This was to make sure that he could have no drugs on him at the time, and also to insure that no drugs could be planted on him by authorities (a common ploy being used in those days in police circles). I know all of this because I was in the car as Ed was being driven to the police station to turn himself in.

When Ed was searched and told to empty his pockets, the authorities were surprised to find that they had been sewn shut. He had nothing on him, and nothing could be planted on him.

Now, as he sat in jail in Baton Rouge, Ed had a lot of time on his hands to think and to come up with some scheme to free himself, and eventually it came to him. He had gotten close enough to Jimmy Hoffa that, whether it was true or not, most people believed he knew a lot about the inner workings of the Teamsters headquarters and its controversial boss. He decided to use this information to his advantage. He wanted out of jail, and he wanted out badly, so he decided to use what he knew (or could convince others he knew) from the Hoffa camp to help himself. He "confessed" to several Baton Rouge officials the details of an alleged plot being planned and said that he had been approached by Jimmy Hoffa to take part in it. Those local officials considered Ed's story to be too hot for them to handle, so they asked if he would be willing to tell it to some Federal agents, and Ed agreed. It was just the opportunity he was looking for.

Legal Charges and Indictments

Federal agents flew to Baton Rouge, and Ed proceeded to tell them about an assassination plot against then-Attorney General Bobby Kennedy. Ed was soon released from prison.

Once out of jail, Ed continued playing his games. He was thinking only of himself and no one else. Ed didn't really have anything on Jimmy Hoffa; He simply used that story to get himself out of jail. To pull it off, he had to convince somebody that he was telling the truth, and he did.

In fact, Ed had agreed to submit to a lie detector test about the assassination attempt on Bobby Kennedy, as I mentioned in an earlier chapter. The test was supposedly administered by the best available technicians, and yet Ed passed the test. I wasn't surprised by this because he had passed similar tests before, when I knew for a fact that he was lying. He had a gift of making a lie sound perfectly believable.

In this case, the government wanted to believe what Ed was saying, and the fact that he passed the polygraph test just gave them a reason to believe him. They were overjoyed that they could now use Ed to get to Hoffa.

But was there such a plot? Personally I don't think Hoffa would have been that stupid, and I doubt very much that he would have asked Ed, of all people, to help him kill Bobby Kennedy, even if he had been planning such an assassination. Hoffa was much smarter than that. He knew that Ed was already in legal trouble of his own and would never have involved him in something so monumental.

Nevertheless, many magazine articles appeared over the coming months alleging that Hoffa had asked Ed to secure a gun with a silencer and get his hands on some plastic explosives, so that he could kill Bobby Kennedy at his compound. Would Jimmy Hoffa have ever trusted Ed to do such crazy things? I never believed it for a moment, and I still don't believe it to this day.

What was it all about then? Ed was just using this whole assassination plot story to get himself out of jail on the kidnapping charges. According to him, he was subjected to several lie detector tests on that subject over the coming months, and he passed them all. But he had always been a consummate liar and, again, could pass any lie detector test. He was a master at it. That's all I can say.

Ed could lie so convincingly on any subject that investigators often took his word for things, without bothering to do any further investigation. He was just that good.

Legal Charges and Indictments

Ed once said that his uncle owned fifteen bars, and those hearing him believed it. But the truth is that no uncle of ours ever owned a bar that I was aware of.

Again, the fact that Federal agents believed Ed's story was only partly his fault. They wanted to believe whatever they heard about Jimmy Hoffa. The lie detector results were enough for them, and they immediately began legal proceedings against the Teamsters leader. So now Ed had painted himself into a corner, and from that point on, he could not turn back. He had to continue the lie, or he would be found out and suffer the consequences. It was all an elaborate fabrication.

I never knew Ed's secret for passing lie detector tests, so don't ask me how he did it. I can only say that he did it, and he did it more than once. I know that for a fact.

An article in *Life* magazine dated May 15, 1964, (Volume 56, No. 20) is very good proof that Ed was a consummate liar. In that article, Ed talked about the rape charges filed against him at an early age. The alleged rape took place on May 1, 1948, and I've already provided the true details of it earlier in the book. What Ed told *Life* was a complete fabrication.

From My Brother's Shadow

In the same article, Ed gave his version of the story of the manslaughter charges filed against him as a result of that automobile accident in Alabama in 1961. I've already provided the true facts of the incident earlier in the book. What Ed told *Life* was a complete fabrication.

The article also included a little information on Ed's very short career in the Marines. As I have stated, he enlisted only as a stipulation of his release from reform school, and his military career was short and undignified. The story he told *Life* was a complete fabrication.

In the *Life* article, Ed also spoke of a boxing career. Well, that was a joke if I ever heard one. I was there, so I know what happened and what didn't, and Ed did not have a boxing career.

Ed also described, in that same article, how he had been elected in 1953 to his position as Secretary-Treasurer/Business Manager of Local #5 in Baton Rouge because, he said, the existing boss, Paul Kuhns, "wanted to retire." These were all lies. Ed was something!

Apparently Jimmy Hoffa was not yet aware of the conversations that had taken place between Ed and representatives of the Federal government because not long afterward Ed was again seen hanging around the Hoffa camp. What was this all about? Ed Partin had now become a snitch for the Federal government, and he was playing his new part to the hilt. His hanging around Hoffa's people was to try to get any information that he could pass along to government investigators. But now Ed was playing with fire. He tried his damnedest to get close to Hoffa and couldn't. The closest Ed ever got to Hoffa was being assigned to watch the door during Hoffa's meetings. He wasn't allowed near Hoffa, not really, not as far as actually being involved in the day-to-day workings of the headquarters. The majority of the information Ed turned over to the government was information he had overheard while sitting in a restaurant or coffee shop near some of Hoffa's key men. No information was ever revealed to him personally. The information he testified to in court, under oath, was either little more than hearsay or even something Ed had thought up himself.

When it was first learned that Ed would testify in court against Jimmy Hoffa, Bobby Kennedy came to Baton Rouge, and Ed and I met with him. At one point in the conversation, Kennedy turned to me and asked, "How do you feel about this, Doug?"

I told him, "I don't like it worth a shit." Those were my exact words. With this, Ed jumped up and told me that I was not to talk to the Attorney General that way. I responded that Mr. Kennedy had asked me a question, and I was just answering him with the truth.

Bobby said it was okay and that I should continue. I told him my fear, for my brother's sake, was that the feds would just use him and then leave him hanging. "When you people get through with Ed Partin, you are going to drop him. You are going to use him and then, when you get through with him, you'll forget about him!" That prediction was to come true, when first John Kennedy was assassinated, and then Bobby Kennedy was assassinated. Now Ed had no one standing in his corner, and he was left out on a limb. He eventually went to prison.

I was against Ed testifying against Hoffa, and he knew that, but of course, he didn't listen to my advice. He was hellbent on being involved in that whole situation, thinking it would take the focus off of him and allow him to escape unscathed. That wasn't to be.

As time passed, I could see things a little more clearly and see exactly where Ed's actions were leading him. He continued to hang around the Hoffa camp, listening and watching and serving as a snitch for the Federal government. This made

Legal Charges and Indictments

Ed, who was boss of a powerful Teamsters local, an enemy of the International Teamsters and its boss.

When Jimmy Hoffa's trial began in Nashville, there were Teamsters agents there from all over the country. They were there to help the man, and they would do anything for him — and I do mean *anything*. That put Ed in a very precarious position. Perhaps Jimmy Hoffa didn't even know about or authorize some of the things his men did to try to help him. They loved him and were ready to do whatever was necessary to get him off.

Ed Partin was there for a totally different reason. He continued to report back to the federal agents assigned over him anything he thought they might like to hear and anything that would help his own case. Some of what Ed reported was factual and meaningful. The many Teamsters agents gathered in Nashville didn't know him and, because they talked freely among themselves of the things that were being done to get Hoffa cleared, their overheard conversations gave Ed fodder to report. Hoffa didn't need to say a word to his troops; they were doing all the dirty work for him.

Personally I am convinced that Jimmy Hoffa was innocent of the charges of bribing a federal juror.

From My Brother's Shadow

He didn't know what his men were doing, whatever government representatives testified. Hoffa had nothing whatsoever to do with what he was being accused of.

Most everyone reading this book will probably have some knowledge of the Hoffa trials, especially those who were living at the time. Some will know more than others. Many of you would probably not be reading this book if you were not in some way interested in the history of the Teamsters and their notorious boss, Jimmy Hoffa. For that reason, I will not go into any of the details about the trials themselves, even though I was present in the courtroom during the Chattanooga trial.

I was present the day Ed was brought in to testify as the government's "surprise witness," and I saw the surprise and shock on Jimmy Hoffa's face when Ed walked in and took his place on the witness stand. I'll never forget that. Those days are branded in my memory forever. Since I wasn't in agreement with what Ed was doing, I was present only as his brother, to lend him my personal support, nothing else.

During that infamous trial, it seemed that everyone was in Chattanooga. The FBI was there in force. Bobby Kennedy was there with his entourage. Walter Sheridan, the famous federal investigator and

Legal Charges and Indictments

confidant of the Kennedy family (Sheridan helped build the case against Hoffa.), was there. On Jimmy Hoffa's side there was the mass of his people from around the country, his lawyers, and his witnesses. And, oh yes, there was that star surprise witness: Edward Grady Partin.

Ed and the U.S. Marshals who now protected him around the clock, were staying at a hotel on the side of Lookout Mountain. Down below, in another hotel, Bobby Kennedy and his FBI team were staying. Kennedy and the FBI agents played football outside the hotel nearly every day.

Both sides were pulling out all the stops. I was even told that Hoffa's people had acquired the services of a man who was very good at reading lips and had him positioned at critical windows with binoculars facing any spot he might be able to catch a glimpse of federal officials and discern their words. Clearly a lot was at stake on both sides, and anything Hoffa and his people could learn about the government's court strategy could be useful to his defense.

Billy Simpson was also in town with Ed and me during the trial. You will remember that it was because Ed had loaned him money and his car to help him get his children out of town and into hiding that he had been charged with kidnapping in the first place. On Friday, February 21, 1964, Billy and I were preparing to leave Chattanooga and go to his home in Alabama. We went to the Greyhound Bus station to see if we could find a bus going in that direction. It was about 11:30 at night, and the next bus to Birmingham was scheduled to leave at 1:55 AM. Having a couple of hours to kill, Billy and I took a cab to a little place called the Farmer's Curb Grill Café.

When we entered the café, there were no other customers. The waitress was the only person in sight. I ordered a glass of milk, and Billy ordered a beer. Within a short time, six or seven other men came in, one or two at a time. Some of them sat at tables, and others sat at the counter. One of the men was familiar to me. I remembered seeing him in the courtroom. He sat down at the counter, next to Billy and me, and started talking. He bought Billy a beer.

Before long this man started arguing with Billy, and it was apparent that he wanted to start a fight. I made Billy change places with me, so that I was sitting between the troublesome man and Billy.

The man kept bragging about how bad and mean he was, trying his best to agitate me. When he finally realized that he could not persuade me to fight, he began calling me a "fed," a "stinking fed," and his language kept getting worse with each accusation. He must have asked me my name at least fifty times, and I told him my name was Westley Foster. He finally came right out and said what was on his mind: "Your name is Partin." At that point, I realized what was going on.

I got up and started toward a phone booth on the other side of the room, but two of the other men who had come in got up and stood between me and the phone booth and refused to let me pass.

There was a phone on the counter where we had been sitting, so I asked permission from the waitress to use it, and she agreed. After I sat back down and started dialing a certain number, the waitress jerked the phone out of my hand and said, "You son of a bitch, we are going to have a party."

At that point one of the other men who had come into the restaurant walked up to Billy and me and put his hands on our shoulders. I guess that was his attempt to keep us in our seats. Then the troublesome man sitting next to me at the counter said, "You g_damn feds. You stinking, dirty feds!" I guess that was when the brawl started.

I was doing pretty well for myself for a while ... until I saw one man coming at me with a cue stick and another man pulling a gun. About the same time I saw the man with the gun, the other man hit me with the cue stick. It sounded like a gunshot, and I thought I had been shot.

The fight must have lasted a pretty good while. I remember regaining consciousness every now and then. One side of my face had hit the concrete floor, and someone was kicking me on the other side of my face. The first man I had hit was lying unconscious under me.

I must have thought they had all left the café, because I roused myself and managed to pull myself up by holding on to the bar stool with one hand and the counter with the other. Eventually I worked my way outside to hunt for Billy.

Billy was nowhere to be seen, so I turned to go back inside the café. I noticed that the first man I had hit was still lying unconscious on the floor, his face covered with blood. I didn't see Billy anywhere. To my surprise, the other men were still inside, and now they jumped me again. I heard them talking as they beat me, saying how damn tough I was, not going down until I was hit with the pool cue.

I managed to work my way outside again, saw a taxi and got my butt into it as fast as I could. But

Legal Charges and Indictments

what about Billy? The driver told me he had seen a man running down the street and going into a phone booth on the corner. We stopped there, and, sure enough, it was Billy. He got in, and we had the taxi take us back to the motel so that I could get myself cleaned up. I got in the shower, clothes and all, but my clothes were so caked with blood and excrement that I had to take a knife and cut them off.

I was banged up pretty badly, so it took me a while, but I finally managed to get myself together, and Billy and I went back to the Greyhound Bus station to buy our bus tickets and begin the trip south. To our surprise, as we were approaching the station, the waitress from the café drove up in a brand new 1962 Pontiac. She got out of the car, came running toward me, and said, "Please! Please! Come here a minute. I've got something you have to hear." She was crying.

When we had gotten closer, she continued, "Please don't tell anyone what I did. If they found me here, they would kill me. You don't know what a chance I'm taking just talking to you. You must really believe in what you're doing because anyone who would fight like you did and take the beating you took is bound to believe in what he's doing!"

From My Brother's Shadow

After thinking more about what the waitress said, I came to the conclusion that she must have been the one who called for the taxi that got us safely away from the café that night. She seemed to be shocked that I had gone back into the café and taken a second beating. Of course, I hadn't been looking for more trouble; I just needed to find Billy. It was later when I realized that Billy had not fought anyone. Instead, he had run out of the café and hid in a damn phone booth. He didn't have a scratch on him.

Billy and I finally reached Birmingham, but we had to catch another bus to Childress, Alabama, where he had a home. When we debarked the bus in Birmingham, there were several Teamsters there, apparently awaiting our arrival. They were probably from the Birmingham local. They were just standing around sneering and watching us. There were two big Teamsters standing beside the door Billy and I had to walk through, and I threatened them. I won't repeat what I said, but they thought I had a gun in my coat, and they quickly deflated. Without further trouble, Billy and I boarded the bus to Childress.

I knew I had been injured in the fight in Chattanooga, and I had been given a number by the FBI to call if I should encounter any trouble, so now I called it. In time, someone came to pick me up, and I was taken to a hospital in Gadsden, about an hour outside of Birmingham, and admitted under an assumed name.

The examination showed that I had sustained a large gash on the top of my head, had several loose teeth, a broken nose and some pretty severe internal injuries. I remained in the hospital for the next several weeks. You've heard the saying, "I'm gonna beat the shit out of you." Well, that's exactly what happened to me. I had the shit beaten out of me. And I couldn't get over the fact that Billy didn't have a scratch on him.

In time, I recovered from my wounds, and soon afterward a few of us Teamsters went back to Chattanooga to "take care of business," but I won't talk about that here.

As it turned out, Billy Simpson had snitched to Hoffa's people about us being in Chattanooga, and Hoffa's people may have thought that I had something to do with Ed testifying against their boss. Or maybe they just wanted to send Ed a message by beating his brother up. I never knew for sure.

Someone later told me that Billy had set me up with Hoffa's people. In time, poor Billy Simpson was assassinated. He answered the door at his home, and someone shot his head off. Some thought I was responsible for Billy's death, but I had absolutely nothing to do with it. The FBI and other Federal government officials knew the full details of these matters.

CHAPTER 6

IMMUNITY AND PROTECTION

When the Hoffa trial was over, Jimmy Hoffa went to prison, and Ed remained a free man, still Principal Officer of Union Local #5 in Baton Rouge. On June 13, 1969, *The Wall Street Journal* (Volume XLIII, Number 116) ran an article by Norman Pearlstine and Herbert G. Lawson pertaining to the Hoffa trial and Ed's role in it. The article stated that Ed had allegedly received a letter from Bobby Kennedy and John Mitchell granting him immunity, in the event he was ever convicted of any of the crimes then charged against him or any future crimes that might be charged against him. Whether or not Ed had such a letter I can't say for sure, but I don't really think so. Knowing Ed as I did (probably better than anyone else), he would definitely have used a letter like that to his advantage.

I believe that the Federal government, including Attorney General Bobby Kennedy, did everything they could possibly do legally to help Ed, but they could only go so far. It was very obvious to all the state and local officials of Louisiana that Ed had a lot of help, and they all knew where that help was coming from. So, for now, Louisiana authorities were unable to touch Ed.

Now that he had testified against Hoffa, Ed enjoyed twenty-four-hour-a-day protection by U.S. Marshals. He loved that.

Personally, I never believed Ed needed to worry about Jimmy Hoffa or his people. I was convinced that having something happen to Ed was the last thing Jimmy Hoffa wanted, because he wanted Ed to recant his testimony against him. He certainly did not want Ed hurt or dead and, thus, unable to recant. There were, however, several alleged attempts on Ed's life, and I need to address those.

You will remember that when Ed was indicted on the kidnapping charges, he had me drive him to

Immunity and Protection

Shreveport and there he caught a plane for Washington, DC. I was under the impression he was on his way to see Hoffa, to ask for his help.

After whatever did or didn't happen in Washington, Ed then returned to Baton Rouge and surrendered himself to authorities. While he was in jail for those charges, he informed local authorities about Hoffa's alleged plot to murder Bobby Kennedy. Calls were made, the wheels started turning, and before long, two federal agents arrived in Baton Rouge to question Ed about the whole affair. Believing Ed's story, those agents made more calls. Bobby Kennedy was warned, and precautions were taken on his behalf. Ed was given a lie detector test, and he passed it with flying colors. So, to avoid staying in jail and facing the tough battle against the kidnapping charges, Ed now promised to cooperate with federal authorities to bring down Jimmy Hoffa.

With some help from the United States government, Ed got out of jail, and he immediately went to work as a snitch, using the undercover name "Andy." Right about then, everyone was after Hoffa big time, so Ed was trying to set Hoffa up and, in the process, score some points for himself.

After Ed was released from jail, it was widely reported that he was working closely with Hoffa. This closeness was purposely being cultivated in his role as government snitch, and continued until shortly before the trial of Hoffa in Nashville began. But these reports were not true because, as I previously stated, Ed was never allowed to get very close to Hoffa. On page 152, in the *Time* magazine photo of Hoffa and his people at the Andrew Jackson Hotel in Nashville, Ed can be seen standing nearby. Believe me, that's about as close as he ever got to Hoffa.

As I noted earlier, most of the information Ed gave to government officials came from conversations he overheard in restaurants and bars, and it seems that some of it may have also come from his own imagination.

The Hoffa trial in Nashville began on October 22, 1962, and ended on December 23, 1962, with a deadlocked jury, and Hoffa was then charged with jury tampering. Little did Hoffa know that Ed , as a government snitch, had played a major role in those jury tampering charges.

Ed returned to Baton Rouge the day after Hoffa's trial ended with that deadlocked jury, and he soon reported an attempt on his life. He was supposedly lying in bed at the Shamrock Motel in Baton Rouge, near the Teamsters local hall, talking on the telephone, when three shots were fired through the window. He stated that he had heard a car stop outside his room and that he had jumped over the foot of the bed to safety just in time to miss the blasts that spread across the bed where he had been lying just moments before.

On another occasion, I received a call from Ossie Brown. I can't remember if he was just an attorney at the time or was already the District Attorney. Anyway, Ossie called me to say that Ed had been shot and told me where he was. I immediately went and picked Ed up and took him to a hospital. There he was treated and sent on to a second hospital. He didn't want anyone to know where he was and what had happened to him.

Here is the truth about those shotgun blasts through the motel window and the truth about Ed's being wounded: Ed actually staged both of those shootings. I know that for a fact. The shooting that took place at the Shamrock Motel was pre-arranged by him, so he knew it was coming, and he was ready for it. Since he was expecting it, all he had to do was play his part.

As far as the incident in which Ed was shot at his apartment, that gunshot wound was self-inflicted. Ed shot himself at close range with a .22 caliber pistol and made sure that he was shot in the fatty part of his abdomen and that the shot missed all of his vital organs. He was not whisked from one hospital to another to protect his identity or keep the media in the dark. I was there with him, and I know. I helped Ed down the back stairs of the hospital and out the back door. Ed simply did not want anyone to discover that he had powder burns on his skin from being shot at close range. This might have revealed that he had shot himself.

All of the media reports on this whole affair consisted only of the facts that Ed wanted printed. Interestingly enough, he eventually "confessed" to authorities that he had accidentally shot himself while moving a loaded gun.

Why did he do it? For one thing, Ed Partin loved attention, especially from the news media. To get it, he got someone to shoot into his room, and then he actually shot himself in the abdomen. He arranged both incidents. I know, for I was there.

The other reason for these fake shootings may have been to make it look as though Jimmy Hoffa were trying to get him. Who knows for sure?

In the early months of 1964, Hoffa, along with several others, was once again in court. This time he was facing the charges of jury tampering. Most everyone interested enough to be reading this book probably followed that trial and knows the story, so again, I will not go into the details of the trial, except to say that most media coverage of it stated that Edward Partin's testimony left Jimmy Hoffa speechless.

I wonder why that would be true. Could it possibly have been because Jimmy Hoffa actually had no knowledge whatsoever that others had tried to bribe jurors on his behalf? Could it possibly have been that Jimmy Hoffa was innocent of jury tampering? Could it possibly have been that the very people who loved and worked so hard to help Hoffa actually hurt him by doing things he knew nothing about? In my opinion, these are all very possible.

On Wednesday, March 4, 1964, Jimmy Hoffa was convicted on two counts of jury tampering in the 1962 trial. He was acquitted on the third count but was still facing eight years in prison.

That first trial against Hoffa began on October 22, 1962 and, as strange as it may seem, that's about the same time that charges and indictments that were then currently pending against Ed Partin began to disappear. In October of that same year, a forgery charge against him was passed, and about a month later the kidnapping charges against him were passed over indefinitely. In December of 1962, other federal charges against Ed were continued indefinitely. About a month after that, a federal court refused to force Ed to answer to the charges involving the death of the soldier in the Alabama car wreck incident. My brother Ed and the news media have told their accounts of what happened in all these events, but now, even though it is many years later, I'm telling the truth about them.

With Donald in
my early years.
*(He's the one
on the left)*

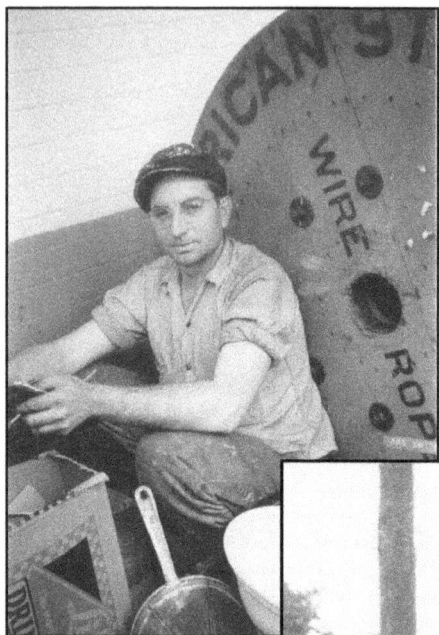

My step-father
Thomas Andrew
Foster

Mother with Andrew
(Left)

The only known photo of my birth father, Grady Edward Partin
(Below)

With my baby sister,
Sandra Ann Foster

Mother and
Sandra Ann

With Mother in Natchez

Me at sixteen

In my Air Force uniform

Donald in his Navy uniform

Donald with our sister Hazel

Mercedes Partin with her daughter, Glenda Gail *(Ed's first child)*

Baby Glenda Gail with our Mother

My brother Ed at various stages of life

1984 file photo/State-Times

Keith Partin, Ed's youngest son and current Principal Officer of Teamsters Local #5

Me as a young Teamster

SHOTGUN BLAST — Teamsters Local 5 member Jimmy Don "Buddy" York checks a shattered storm door at the rear of his home after a shotgun blast ripped through the house last night. York had returned from a union meeting and gone to bed shortly before buckshot entered the front of the house and penetrated walls and doors before smashing out of the back door, he said. Teamster construction workers had two meetings at their union hall Monday night at which members said discontent was aired. Teamster Business Manager Edward G. Partin, below center, is serving a federal prison term in Texas. Acting Business Manager Doug Partin, below right, and Assistant Business Agent and Recording Secretary Allen Jones below left, left the hall after the first meeting Monday.

— Photo by Charles Gerald

Teamsters gather outside hall before arguing about Partin's fate

Teamsters dissident leader Jimmy Don "Buddy" York

Ed alongside Jimmy Hoffa outside the Andrew Jackson Hotel in Nashville (*This was as close as he got to Hoffa.*)

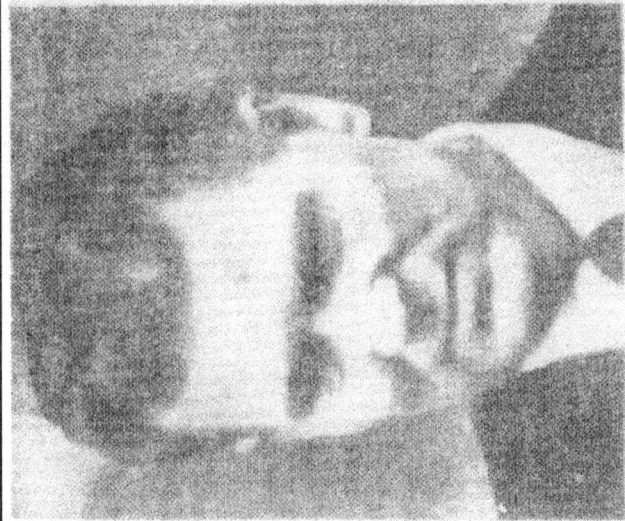

ACCUSER AND ACCUSED — Edward Grady Partin, left, business manager of the Baton Rouge local of the Teamsters union, has become the chief government witness in the trial of his boss, President James R. Hoffa, right, in Chattanooga, Tenn. Hoffa is being tried on jury tampering charges.
—AP wirephoto.

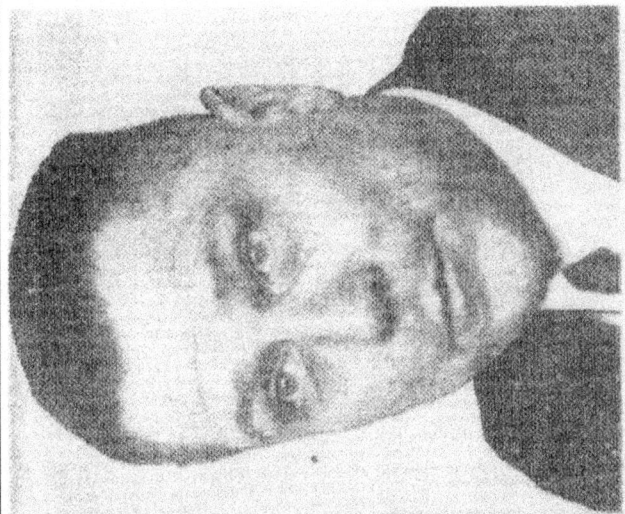

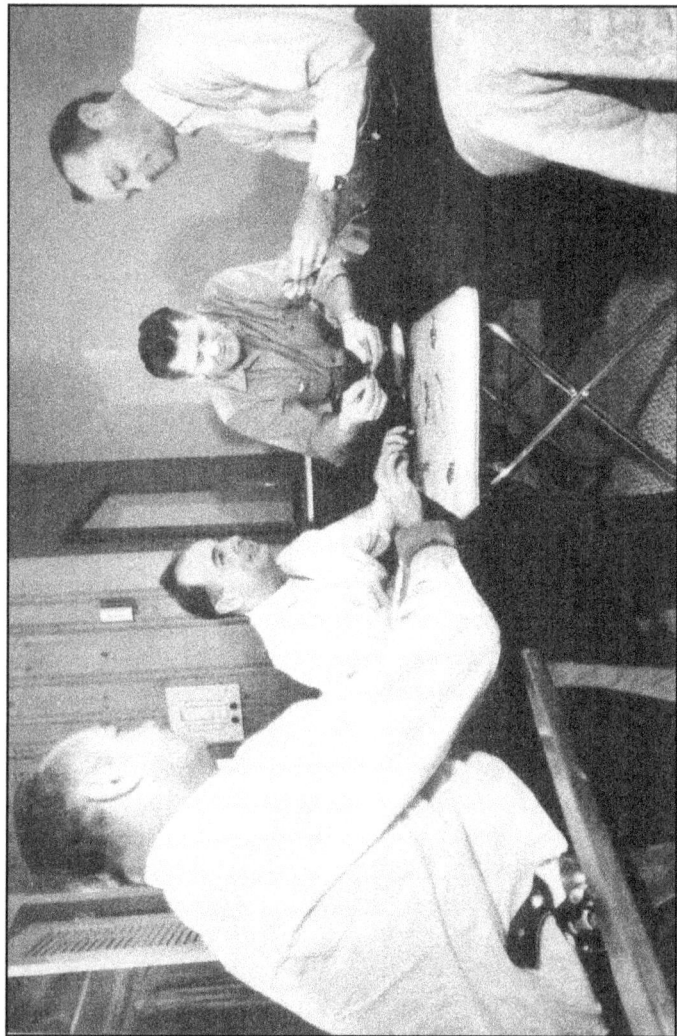

Ed and Emmett Tucker in a hotel in Chattanooga flanked by the U.S. Marshals protecting them

A Life magazine photo
of Emmett at the motel
in Chattanooga
*(No one was supposed to know
where they were hidden)*

Uncle Doug,

Jennifer, my daughter, wrote this in school almost 2 months ago. She put it in Daddy's pocket, along with Jamie's letter.

I never really knew my grandfather.
His whole life is a mystery to me.
For he ended up being a brother
To Nejra and a good friend to Kennedy.
The only way I learned about his past
Was from reading his magazines and books.
Now time is flying by so very fast,
And I am afraid I will never look
At his tender and loving face again.
For he is extremely ill and near death.
Lord, when he dies, his new life will begin.
So give him mercy, for he tried his best.
I know he'll go to the heavens above
And look down upon me and feel my love.

To Big Daddy
from your loving grandaughter,
Jennifer
January 1990

Jan. 10, 1975
Dec. 15, 1975

Dear Brother Odom & Wife:

I want to thank you for the wonderful scripture on the xmas card and the beautiful xmas card.

Thank you very much. It was a pleasant honor to receive it.

I am so proud that God saw fit to give me the opportunity to be a Christian at Parkview. They are such wonderful thoughtful Christians and I love them.

The Lord has given me peace of mind and happiness that can't be explained in words. Thank God. A great burden was lifted off my shoulders and my families.

Meary xmas to both of you and a happy new year and many more after that. God bless you and your family.

In Christ Love
Ed Partin

P. S. Thanks for thinking of me words cannot express it.

A letter Ed wrote from prison to a Baptist pastor and his wife

Donald and
his wife Vivian
(Left)

In my office at
the Local Hall
(Bottom)

Ed with
Mother
(Left)

Me with Mother
(Bottom)

With Sandy, the love of my life

CHAPTER 7

BACK TO BUSINESS AS USUAL

The trial of Jimmy Hoffa in Chattanooga had ended, and he was awaiting appeal, but the whole event had been so publicized that it now left Ed's future with the local in Baton Rouge in doubt. On March 9, 1964, Ed stood before a crowd of some two hundred and fifty Teamsters in the Baton Rouge Teamsters hall and called for a vote of confidence. He had just gotten back from the trial, he told the men present that night that they should expect trouble from Hoffa and his men. Without elaborating, he told them that he had already experienced trouble from the Teamsters boss, and that they could expect much more of it if he were kept on as boss of the local. It was important to him, he said, to know exactly how the members felt about him. If they were no longer satisfied with him, he would step down from his position with the union. No one was surprised when Ed received a full vote of confidence from the union members to continue his work at Teamsters Union Local #5.

Until that night, the union hall in Baton Rouge had been known as "Hoffa Hall," but that now changed, and the photo of Jimmy Hoffa that had hung predominantly in the hall for many years was taken down and placed somewhere out of sight.

About two weeks later, there was an article in an Alexandria, Louisiana, newspaper stating that Ed had said Hoffa would be out as the Teamsters boss if he had to serve a jail sentence. Ed wanted Hoffa out of office badly, for he knew that if Hoffa stayed in office, sooner or later Hoffa would find a way to take the Baton Rouge local over under trusteeship, which meant that the International Brotherhood of Teamsters Union would appoint someone else to Ed's position to run the local. Ed feared this, and so he did everything he possibly could to keep Hoffa in jail.

Back to Business As Usual

Personally I believe that Jimmy Hoffa was a good leader, and I always liked him. He made some mistakes during his reign over the Teamsters union, but back in those days you had to make deals with anyone you could.

Jimmy Hoffa was able to get the National Master Freight Agreement through the mob, and that was a major victory, for the mob controlled a lot of the freight lines. As part of the deal, Hoffa loaned the mob money from the Teamsters' pension fund. These funds were invested in the casinos in Las Vegas, and this turned out to be a very good investment for the Teamsters' pension fund. But now, Jimmy Hoffa was in prison, Ed was back to his old tricks, and I was right there taking it all in.

Not everything in life revolved around the Teamsters. It wasn't long after Hoffa went to jail that our father, Grady Edward Partin, passed away. He had been suffering for some time with lung cancer. The period of his illness was a very difficult one for me personally. There were many decisions that needed to be made regarding his care during his final days, and I was the one who had to make them. I made the difficult decisions and followed through with them, and I am now comfortable and at peace with what I decided.

From My Brother's Shadow

Our father died on April 14, 1967, and soon afterward, Ed gave away everything Daddy had owned to other people. He did not want Donald, Hazel or me to have anything that was sentimental to us.

For some strange reason, Ed had always wanted our parents to himself. He didn't want the rest of us to have anything to do with either Daddy or Mother.

Just to give you an idea of what I mean: Ed had Mother living near him one time, and he had a tenfoot cyclone fence erected around the house and land where she lived, and she and Ed were the only ones allowed to have a key to the gate. He didn't even want the rest of us to visit her. In some ways, he was a very weird person, and he had some very odd ways about him. During the time Mother lived there, the only way I could visit her was to climb over that ten-foot cyclone fence.

Mother was often overly concerned about Ed, and one time she actually called Bobby Kennedy to ask for his help. Surprisingly, Bobby Kennedy talked to her. I guess she felt she could call him anytime she wanted because she thought he owed her family, and I guess maybe he did. If it hadn't been for Ed, Kennedy would never have been able to convict Jimmy Hoffa.

Back to Business As Usual

Ed had always had the reputation of being a tough Teamster leader, and now that he was back in Baton Rouge from the trial, that reputation took on a whole new dimension. Ed took full advantage of his vote of confidence and continued with business as usual, and I continued observing from his shadow.

Along about then, things started to heat up in Baton Rouge and the surrounding areas. I don't know for sure, but this may have been because Ed was craving more attention and recognition after the Hoffa trial. After all, he had become a national hero of sorts, helping the federal government get Jimmy Hoffa. He was a big man now, and I just remained in his shadow, taking care of business.

I remember well an incident that happened about then which involved some labor violence on the W.O. Bergeron construction site in Plaquemine, Louisiana, on January 17, 1968. I can't help but laugh now, thinking back, but at the time it was no laughing matter. There was some serious stuff going on at that job site, and other Teamsters and I were trying to "get out of Dodge," as the old saying goes.

A group of us, three or four in front and six or eight in back, were riding in a pickup truck, hightailing it out of town. I was with those in the back.

From My Brother's Shadow

Someone shooting at us had shot a hole in the bottom of the gas tank, and, because of that hole, we were quickly running out of gas. For some reason, we had a five-gallon can of gas in the back of the truck, and I proceeded to take that five-gallon can of gas, lean out over the side of the truck, and pour gas into the tank as we were moving, hoping somehow that it would be enough to get us out of town. Thinking back on that incident, we must have been a funny-looking group going down the road, but it was not funny at the time. We finally made it out of Plaquemine without the state police catching us, but some of the other Teamsters did get caught and were arrested. Later, everyone labeled that incident as "The Shoot-out at the OK Corral."

This is what really happened that day: A group of us Teamsters went out to the Bergeron construction site that day, and the workers on site were ready for us. We proceeded to walk around the site, and the workers started shooting at us. They were down in ditches they had dug to install sewage pipe in, so they were pretty well protected, as they shot at us. However, we were unarmed and out in the open, and they were shooting our asses off. All of us Teamsters ran back to our cars and trucks and got our guns, and the "OK Corral Shoot-out" was on.

Back to Business As Usual

A couple of our Teamsters were shot pretty badly that day. We took them to Gloster, Mississippi, to a doctor we knew there, and he took the bullets out of them and patched them up. That was not the first time. The same doctor had patched up a few other Teamsters over the years. He was there for us when we needed him.

The story behind that whole W.O. Bergeron incident in Plaquemine was that Bergeron was using concrete pipe made by a non-union company called Stevens Concrete Pipe. For this reason, Teamsters Union Local #5 members went out on the job site to set up a picket line. We were trying to get W.O. Bergeron to use union-made pipe, but it did not work out that way.

About ten Teamsters were arrested as a result of the "OK Corral" incident, and there just so happened to be a new attorney in the Baton Rouge area, and they hired him. His name was Paul Thompson, and this was his first case.

Hearing the facts of the case, Paul came to the conclusion that this would be a cakewalk and that he "had it made." He went to the courthouse, thinking the cases were going to be a local court deal, but when he entered the courtroom and saw FBI agents, U.S. Attorneys and the District Attorney present, all representing the case for the government, he had another think coming. He later stated, "My first ten cases, and I lost all of them. It taught me a lesson, not to ever represent the Teamsters again!"

New charges were lodged against Ed. As noted earlier, rumor had it that he enjoyed blanket immunity against past and future prosecution, because of his testimony against Jimmy Hoffa. Other rumors were also flying around that Ed had been approached by some to recant his testimony against Hoffa. That was something the federal government certainly did not want to happen. Everyone knew that Ed had friends and supporters in the Justice Department. Of course, Ed denied it, but he continued to enjoy the twenty-four-hour-a-day U.S. Marshal protection.

According to Ed, he was offered several bribes to recant his testimony against Hoffa. One of those bribes was offered through Carlos Marcello, mob boss in New Orleans. Several other people tried to get in touch with Ed to persuade him to recant his testimony, including one judge, but Ed was never willing to take back what he had testified against Jimmy Hoffa. He had too much to lose.

At one point, it looked like Ed's recantation would take place. He was scheduled to meet some people at the Teamsters hall to recant, but Ed changed his mind and sent all the employees in the hall home. He then had a note placed on the door of the hall stating that our mother had passed away and including funeral arrangement details. There is a little more to that story, and I'll get into it a little later in the book.

Emboldened, Ed continued to do as he damn well pleased, both in his personal actions, as well as in union business matters. He was something else. I was there, and I witnessed it all. After so many years, Ed continued to believe that he could do no wrong and that he could have anything he wanted for the taking. He didn't care who was hurt in the process, who was killed or who went to prison. Many Teamsters went to jail for Ed Partin.

In the late 1960s Ed led everyone to believe that his health was beginning to fail. Over the next three or four years, he became less and less active in union business and finally took a leave of absence from the local on February 23, 1970. It was at that point in time that I became more active at Local #5. I was asked to step into the position of Business Agent, and this was voted on and passed by the Executive Board and general membership of the local. Ed continued to be the principal officer for the following eight or nine years, and it was considered that I was simply filling in for him, but I was doing all the work.

Because Ed had not been active in union business that year (1970), he was not paid a salary for the entire year. I, on the other hand, was active at the hall, tackling union business. After all those years of being kept in Ed's shadow as I watched him at work, I was now stepping out of his shadow and facing head-on the challenges that presented themselves to me. And, believe me, there were many challenges ahead of me that I had not anticipated.

Ed was in and out of court on various charges during those years. In the late 1970s, he faced a charge of conspiracy to obstruct justice. That was the straw that finally broke the proverbial camel's back. It was this charge that finally brought Ed down.

During this time, Ed filed bankruptcy to protect his assets. He owed a lot of money and thought he was about to be sued. In his bankruptcy claim, he cited the fact that he was not then receiving a salary. The bankruptcy settlement took several years, but when everything had finally been settled, Ed decided that he wanted those years of back salary he hadn't been paid from the union. And you know what? As crazy as that sounds, Ed got those years of back pay.

Back to Business As Usual

Then, after getting years of back salary from the union, Ed refused to pay the income taxes on all that money. He insisted that the local had to pay the taxes for him.

Ed had not changed. He knew how to control things and how to use his power to maximum advantage. Whatever Ed wanted, the Executive Board and membership would give. I had seen Ed stand up brazenly at union meetings and try to get elected as local union boss, not just for three years, as the Teamsters constitution stated, but for life. These attempts were not successful, but that didn't stop him from trying. Everyone was afraid of him, and they all wanted to look good to him, so this gave him an incredible amount of control.

As noted much earlier in the book, for some years he had control of most of the construction work in and around Baton Rouge. For the first few years after he had initially gone to the capital city, he had been very well liked, and he really did well. The local politicians liked to be seen with him. His popularity began to decline as he got greedier and started abusing his power.

But that was just Ed being Ed. He had power, and he was going to exercise it. Politicians all appreciated the power he had, and Ed took care of some of them, making sure they had enough money to run for re-election. Now, gradually, his power was also beginning to decline.

CHAPTER 8

TWO MYSTERIOUS PLANE CRASHES

A very interesting article, written by Larry Dickerson, appeared in the *State Times* newspaper of Baton Rouge, on June 1, 1971, about the plane crash in which the famous Audie Murphy lost his life. Had someone wanted Audie Murphy out of the way? I can't say for sure. I do know that Audie and Ed had been hanging around together a lot. I also know that Audie associated with a man by the name of D'Alton Smith, who was the son-in-law of noted New Orleans mob boss Carlos Marcello. D'Alton was in cahoots with Marcello and had been instrumental in trying to get Ed to recant his testimony against Jimmy Hoffa, offering Ed money (among other things). I don't know if D'Alton Smith had anything to do with Audie Murphy's death or not. I do, however, know that Audie Murphy was working for Jimmy Hoffa. I also know for a fact that Audie Murphy was talking to Ed and trying to persuade him to recant the testimony against Hoffa. Rumors at the time were that Audie and Ed were contemplating some type of business venture together, with the help of Jimmy Hoffa. Personally, I think that was all some sort of cover for the fact that they spent so much time together. I don't know if Hoffa had anything to do with all of this or not. It was all circumstantial.

It would be hard to say whether or not Ed was aware that the plane that Audie Murphy was on was going to crash. What I can say is that Ed was scheduled to be on that same flight but canceled at the last minute, giving the excuse that his wife was ill, so he couldn't make the trip. I can tell you, in all sincerity, that Ed's wife being sick would *never* have stopped him from boarding any flight to anywhere he really wanted to go.

There was another mysterious plane crash that was not as widely publicized as the Audie Murphy crash. I knew the people involved. During Ed's reign

Two Mysterious Plane Crashes

as Boss, Teamsters Union Local #5 in Baton Rouge had the reputation of being one of the toughest locals in the entire nation — and with good reason.

The second plane crash I want to tell you about was a result, I believe, of one of Ed's business ventures that few people knew about, one of his many money-making schemes.

I know for a fact that, at one time, a Teamster by the name of Jerry Sylvester had a racetrack registered in his name. That racetrack actually belonged to Ed, but Ed didn't want anyone to know that he owned it. A little time passed and, at Ed's request, Jerry transferred ownership of the track into our Mother's name. Remember that Mother had remarried, and her name was no longer Partin, but Foster. As often happened, Ed had become suspicious of Jerry and no longer wanted him to be associated with the track, so he had him put the track in Mother's name.

The thing that turned Ed off to Jerry Sylvester was the rumor that Jerry was somehow involved with the federal government. How deep he was involved no one could say, but when Ed heard about that, he marginalized the man immediately. He didn't want to take the chance that Jerry would snitch on him to the feds or testify against him in court.

The track in question was not some dinky little

dirt track; it was a beautiful NASCAR-type racetrack. Ed had named it the Baton Rouge International Speedway, and Donny and Bobby Allison, Red Farmer and many other famous NASCAR drivers came to Prairieville, Louisiana (just south of Baton Rouge) and raced there.

Another reason Ed wanted to keep his ownership of the track secret was that many of the materials for its construction had come from Texaco job sites, and several contractors were involved in building it, and nothing had cost Ed a single dime. Dunham Ready Mix and Concrete Pipe Company had put up a lot of money and had poured all the concrete on the site, and Ed didn't pay for any of that. I was there, and I saw what happened.

One serious problem with the whole project was that the people of Baton Rouge and the surrounding areas were crazy about football and not so crazy about car racing, and so, after the track was built, there were not enough fans to support it, and it failed financially.

Ed decided to sell the entire facility, and he came up with a buyer out of Texas who wanted to purchase it. There was just one catch: the buyer wanted proof that the racetrack was drawing enough crowds to sustain such a facility. Ed came up with an imaginative idea. He had several thousand tickets printed up and then he gave them away in the area schools. Anyone who wanted to come to the track could come free. Consequently the crowds were standing-room-only when the prospective buyer from Texas flew to Baton Rouge in his private jet. After seeing the large crowds at Baton Rouge International Speedway, he bought it. Ed had pulled off another of his sleazy deals.

Jerry Sylvester, in whose name the racetrack had originally been titled, was a pilot and owned his own plane. He and his brother-in-law had gone on a trip in that plane and had experienced some sort of problem with it and could not use it to get home. Another pilot friend of ours, Paul Littlefield, loaned Jerry his plane for their trip home. After they had gotten airborne, the plane's engine failed, and Jerry could not get it restarted or gain control over the falling plane before it hit the ground. Both Jerry and his brother-in-law were killed in the resulting crash.

This crash happened on the outskirts of Clinton, Louisiana. Paul Littlefield, the plane's owner, was a game warden for the State of Louisiana, and he often flew us to other states and could land his plane in a cornfield or on some other rough landing strip. Together, we would also do things for other Teamsters officials and then come back to Baton Rouge, just as though we had never left town. Paul had his own landing strip in his backyard in Clinton, so no one knew when he was flying out or when he was flying back in.

Paul had never before taken a drink in his life, but the day he loaned Jerry Sylvester his plane, and it crashed, killing Jerry and his brother-in-law, Paul started drinking. He drank until the day he died (of liver problems from all the drinking).

Paul Littlefield and I were very good friends. In fact, at one time, he offered to give me some property in Arkansas on a beautiful lake, but I declined to accept it. Paul and Ed were close, too. Jerry Sylvester was also a friend of mine and just so happened to be dating a very close friend of mine at the time of his death. So this whole episode was very painful for me, aside from being so very mysterious.

As for the Baton Rouge International Speedway, under the new ownership, it was renamed Pelican International Speedway, Inc., but it never did very well. I have in my possession a three-page letter dated January 13, 1971, under the heading Pelican International Speedway, Inc., MacDonald Lynch, from Mineral Wells, Texas. The letter refers to an

Two Mysterious Plane Crashes

offer made to me to manage the racetrack. I seriously considered their management proposal, but in the end, I turned it down. That track didn't seem to have much of a future.

CHAPTER 9

ED FINALLY GOES TO JAIL

Over the next seven or eight years, the local newspapers and television stations in Baton Rouge, as well as some national media, had their hands full trying to keep up with the goings-on of Edward Grady Partin. Hardly a week went by that he was not in the news somehow. It was anything from interesting local union news to Ed trying to cover his butt legally.

Jimmy Hoffa was still making the news as well, wanting to take back his former position with the Teamsters, so I can only suppose that Hoffa also continued to have hopes of convincing or persuading Ed to recant his testimony against him. Yeah! Right! Maybe when hell freezes over.

From My Brother's Shadow

As I noted in previous chapters, the charges that eventually sent Ed to prison were conspiracy to obstruct justice and, later, misappropriation of union funds. Ed was convicted in November of 1977 on three counts of conspiracy to obstruct justice by hiding government witnesses against him in an earlier trial in Houston, Texas. Judge Naumann Scott of Alexandria, Louisiana, sentenced Ed to three four-year terms in a federal penitentiary, two of which were to run concurrently. The type of sentences Ed was given made him eligible for parole at any time federal parole authorities deemed him fit.

I was there, and I heard and saw it all. In June of 1980, Ed and I were together in San Diego, California, for his court appearance, to determine if and when he would begin serving his sentence. According to Ed's conversation with me, he had bribed the judge and knew the outcome of the case. He told me that he had given the judge $25,000 in cash and that the judge was going to set him free, putting him on probation, so that he would not be going to jail at all. This time, Ed was dead wrong.

When Ed and I boarded the plane in New Orleans for the trip to San Diego, I saw a man walking through the airport to board the same plane, and he was flashing a badge as he boarded. I told Ed I thought the man was an FBI agent, but Ed didn't seem to think so. I just answered, "Okay."

Then, when we arrived in the courtroom in San Diego on Monday, June 23, 1980, guess who was sitting there in the courtroom? It was the same man who had flashed his badge while boarding the plane with us in New Orleans. I pointed the man out once again to Ed and told him that something was going on. Ed still insisted that we didn't have anything to worry about, that he had already taken care of the judge. I told him things sure didn't look all that good to me.

Ed's case had been scheduled to be heard that day, but, for some reason, court recessed about 10:00 AM for the day, and we were told to return to court the following morning. Ed and I went back to our hotel, and that night Ed asked me to call Walter Sheridan. As you might remember, Sheridan was the special assistant to Bobby Kennedy during the Hoffa trial.

I located Walter Sheridan in Washington, DC, and told him that something strange was going on in San Diego. He said to me, "You tell Ed Partin that I said he is going to be incarcerated in San Diego, in a federal correctional facility, and he is going to be a prisoner. And you tell him that he'd better start acting like a prisoner." And, with that, he abruptly hung up.

From My Brother's Shadow

I hung up the phone on my end and went and told Ed exactly, word for word, what Sheridan had said. To say the very least, Ed was upset and began telling me, over and over, to get Sheridan back on the phone.

I was able to reach Sheridan again, and this time I handed the phone to Ed, so that he could hear the news firsthand. It was in that moment that Ed realized for the first time that he was really going to prison. The news shook him.

Somehow Ed had always believed he would never do serious jail time. He had gotten off so many times and done what he wanted when he wanted without seeming to pay any consequences, that now he was in shock. He had been very serious when he described to me how he had bought his way out of jail, but this time it hadn't worked.

With my own eyes, I had seen Ed hand a lawyer, who was reputed to be close to this judge, $25,000 in cash. That lawyer later told Ed that he hadn't been able to do anything for him and that he didn't need the money, but Ed insisted that he keep it. And he walked out of the lawyer's office that day, leaving the money with the lawyer, simply because he believed the lawyer was a friend of the judge and would do what needed to be done. But it hadn't worked.

The next day after the phone conversation with Walter Sheridan, we were called back to the courtroom to take up Ed's case. It was the only case on the court docket for that day, and it didn't take the judge long to sentence Ed to twelve years in prison. Ed was taken from the courtroom in handcuffs and went directly to jail.

Before he was led away that day, police officials allowed Ed to write out a statement to Weldon Mathis, International Vice-President at Teamsters headquarters in Washington, DC, placing me in charge of Teamsters Local #5 while Ed was incarcerated. I have a copy of that handwritten letter in my possession. It reads:

Weldon Mathis

Dear Sir and Brother,

I have some problems that are going to keep me busy at least until August 20th. My brother Douglas, who is an officer of the local and a longtime member, will be acting on a day-to-day basis to see to it that things are carried on according to your wishes and the international and the local #5 and me. With your permission, I will get him to handle my business with Stone and Webster in my absence, because he is thoroughly familiar with it. I will be in touch with you on most matters.

Fraternally,

E.G. Partin
Business Mgr. & Sec'y. Treas.

The letter was then typed up on Local #5 letterhead, dated June 23, 1980, and forwarded to Mr. Weldon Mathis.

On June 27, 1980, an article appeared in a local Baton Rouge newspaper, *State Times,* which stated: "PARTIN STARTS EIGHT-YEAR TERM IN SAN DIEGO FOR CONSPIRACY TO OBSTRUCT JUSTICE." It pointed out that Ed had been in that same federal penal institution once before, on a six-month contempt of court sentence. It also stated that the high-rise building that housed the prison had been built in 1974, had a staff of 160 and could house 450 men and women. It also stated that the facility offered an environment free of steel grills, high noise levels and stark surroundings. I thought it was one of the most interesting articles among the many that appeared in local newspapers in the days after Ed was finally incarcerated. The San Diego facility was described by some as resembling a bank rather than a prison and with the amenities of some of the finer hotels. Ed was now the major topic of conversation around the Baton Rouge area and remained so for quite a while.

And that was how Edward Grady Partin went to prison. As his brother, I knew some things. In fact, I knew a lot of things, but I would never have talked. Never! Ever! I was called before grand juries twice, but I could not be persuaded to say anything against my brother.

Yes, that brother had tried to have me killed. He had also tried to have me indicted (all of which I will get to a little further along in my story). It had been a wild ride, but I stuck by him through it all. No matter what he had done to me, he was my brother.

Ed had been fearful of going to prison for years before he actually went. As I look back on it now, I should have known that it was inevitable that he would one day wind up behind bars. As his brother,

From My Brother's Shadow

I certainly didn't want him to be there, no matter what some family members and so-called friends may have thought. Over the years, I had done my best to help him and keep him out of trouble and out of prison.

For instance, there was my trip to Africa. Actually I made two trips on his behalf. Ed wanted to get a passport because he was afraid he was going to prison, and so he was making plans to skip the country, and he wanted a fake passport in another name. I went to Algeria twice, once in July and once in August of 1970, but was unable to get the desired passport.

My purpose in going to Algeria was to meet with Huey Newton, a Black Panther who had killed some policemen in a shoot-out in California. After the shoot-out, Newton fled to Cuba to live, but he often traveled to Algeria, at the time a Communist country. When I visited him there, he was staying in a large hacienda with maids and many other amenities. We had heard that he could secure illegal passports, and I went there to get one for Ed, but Huey Newton could not (or would not) help us.

Part of this could have been Ed's fault. I had told him that in order to get a passport for him I would need a photo ID of him, and he stubbornly refused to give it to me.

On that first trip in July, I was required to wait in Spain for about two weeks for my visa to Algeria. Because of the Communist influence in the country, Americans needed a visa in order to get in there. Then, because I didn't have a photo ID of Ed for the passport, I had to fly all the way back to Baton Rouge and then fly back to Algeria again. I went through some scary moments doing all of this.

I had thought that the visa I secured was good anytime once you got it, so, on the second trip, I went on into Algeria on the original visa, not knowing that I was supposed to have gotten a new one. The result was that I nearly did not get out of that country. What a scary situation that was for me! Still, despite having made two trips, I was unable to secure the passport Ed required. My contacts had been of no help.

Ed had worried so much about going to prison that he already had a false identification card for Mexico with his photo on it. His family name on the card was given as "Gonzales." He had wanted the passport to go on from Mexico into some other country, to elude the U.S. authorities. I never knew where, how long or how Ed was planning to live in some other place or how he could afford to live there after his initial money had run out, but I'm sure, knowing Ed, that he had made contingency plans.

Trying to get the passport was just one of the many crazy things I was called upon to do over the years for my brother. Some people don't even believe me about the two trips to Algeria, so I know they wouldn't believe the rest.

It's a true story, and I have to this day my stamped passport showing my entry and exit from Algeria. The passport in question was issued to me on June 30, 1970, and the expiration date on it was June 29, 1975. That was one hell of a trip, and the only trip that I made with that particular passport.

CHAPTER 10

ED WORKS AGAINST ME FROM PRISON

The year was 1980, and I had taken a few more steps out of Ed's shadow and was taking care of Teamsters Local #5 business on a daily basis, as I had been asked and instructed to do by Ed himself. Ed was in prison, and I was taking care of day-to-day union local business, but he continued to want total control. He still did not want me to have any major say-so when it came to important decisions, even though he could not be anywhere near the local offices at the time. It took me a while, but I finally figured out what he was doing.

The very first time I realized that Ed was undermining me and trying to hurt me from his prison cell was when I was working on organizing the Coca-Cola Bottling Company in Baton Rouge.

There was a newspaper article printed on August 12, 1980, in the *Morning Advocate*, a Baton Rouge newspaper, pertaining to that strike. It stated that Ed was trying to control the strike from prison. I came to find out that my own executive board was working with him and against me, trying to make the Coca-Cola picket line fail. Even my own recording secretary on the executive board was working with the opposition, informing the Coca-Cola Company's attorney of our daily plans for following the Coca-Cola trucks, including the days and times we would be following them around the city, and where we would be putting up picket signs.

I learned from a friend who used the same attorney as the Coca-Cola Bottling Company that Ed was giving specific instructions, from prison, to certain Teamsters executive board members on how to undermine me. Subsequently those members voted, in an executive board meeting, to cut off the funds I needed to support the picket-line workers involved in the strike. This was when I first came to realize that Ed was actually working against me. I guess I shouldn't have been surprised.

Even after Ed had gone to prison, I continued to give him credit for everything. I was constantly being asked

Ed Works Against Me from Prison

questions by the news media, and I would answer that I would have Ed call them. If you don't believe me, read the newspaper article in the *State Times* of Baton Rouge printed July 3, 1980. I preferred to stay in the background. That way I wouldn't be caught up in the limelight.

Ed was just the opposite. He loved the news media attention, and that was just fine and dandy with me. So I let him have it all.

Another article in the Baton Rouge *Morning Advocate*, dated Thursday, May 28, 1981, revealed another of Ed's attempts to undermine me. The article described how a worker had been ordered to stay away from the union hall. The worker's name was Glynn J. O'Banion, and he had been instructed by Ed to create some problems. Apparently, Ed had either given or mailed O'Banion a letter telling him that he was to take charge of Teamsters Local #5.

O'Banion was really something; he had more guts than any other human being I'd ever met. He had already shot and wounded a fellow Teamster in a prior incident. Now he came strolling into the Teamsters hall with his letter from Ed. He handed me the letter and proceeded to announce to all the Teamsters present in the hall that day that Ed Partin had put him in charge of Local #5.

From My Brother's Shadow

I opened the letter and read it, instantly recognizing Ed's handwriting and signature. When I had finished, I handed O'Banion back his letter and said, "You know what you can do with this letter." He turned and left the union hall. I later heard that Glynn O'Banion was dead. Apparently he had fallen from a tree.

I have in my possession several letters written by Ed from prison. I will not disclose to whom the letters were written. I will only say that they were not written to me. The return address on the letters was E.G Partin, Camp #2, Post Office Box 1000, LaTuna, Anthony, New Mexico/Texas, and the postmark on the letters was Anthony, New Mexico/Texas.

The following excerpt is from one of those letters, and I have inserted some notes into the body of the letter explaining Ed's comments:

Thursday Evening
June 25, 1981

Dear _____,

I just finished talking to you on the phone. I appreciate everything that the men have ever done for me on helping with the attorneys. Without them I could have never

Ed Works Against Me from Prison

made it. I sure hope that everything was voluntary, because it would break my heart to think that someone didn't do it because they wanted to. **[Note: Here Ed is referring to the money being taken up on the jobs for him. When I took over, I stopped the practice of demanding it, so if any was taken up, it had to be voluntary, and I knew nothing about it.]** I broke down and cried when I heard what you told me. I am here because of the members. **[Note: Ed blamed the Teamsters members for his incarceration, but they had nothing to do with his being in prison. He was convicted of conspiracy and embezzlement of union funds.]** I have given my life for Local #5, and I never thought I would see the day it would be any argument over helping any person in trouble. I have never talked to anyone in my life about it, and I thought all the time the people were helping me because they cared. I just wish I had a preacher I could talk to tonight. I don't believe I have ever felt this bad in my life. I don't believe the members know what torment all of us have went through for that local.

Please get some of the old timers to drop me a line. I sure feel low tonight.

From My Brother's Shadow

Tell everyone I said hello.

Fraternally,
Your Friend, Ed Partin

Ed was something. He always wanted things done his way, but there were some things I just had to do the right way, the correct way and the fair way for all involved.

For instance, on Tuesday morning, October 13, 1981, the headlines of the *Advocate* newspaper in Baton Rouge read TEAMSTERS TO VOTE ON PARTIN OUSTER. That was all about issuing Ed a withdrawal card, and I want to tell you the true facts about that incident:

Ed was in prison, still serving time, and there was a man by the name of Hugh Marionneaux who, at one time, had been the president of Teamsters Local #5. Hugh had gone to prison, too. And when Hugh went to prison, Ed issued him a withdrawal card, in accordance with the constitution of the Teamsters. Ed was right in doing what he did. So, now, when Ed was in prison and not working for the union, Hugh Marionneaux insisted that Ed be issued a withdrawal card, just as *he* had been. And Hugh Marionneaux was correct to request this.

Ed Works Against Me from Prison

I had not issued Ed a withdrawal card until then because I hated to do it. He was my brother, I knew more than anyone what Local #5 meant to him, and I didn't want to hurt him. So I had just been letting the issue ride. However, the Teamsters members were on my butt big time about the matter and were considering filing charges against *me* because of it. They were becoming very angry over this issue, and Ed was now the main topic of conversation every day. His withdrawal card, his salary, his Continental automobile, and the house he had at the time were all sore subjects around the union. All of this was bound to come to a head, and the sad thing was the Teamsters of Local #5 were right about the whole thing. I realized it was time to do something. I just wanted to do it right.

I knew I had to go see Ed in person and explain to him what had to be done and why, so that's what I did. Ed had been transferred to that prison on the Texas/New Mexico border, so that's where I now went. I took two members of the Local #5 executive board with me, as witnesses. I knew this would be a very difficult thing for Ed, so I was not about to mail him a withdrawal card. I hand-delivered it, in the hope that, if I sat down with him and explained everything, this might remove some of the sting. Surely he would be able to see our viewpoint.

From My Brother's Shadow

When I arrived and asked to see Ed, I was told that he was meeting with Gordon Pugh, the attorney for the City of Baton Rouge. When they were finished, I got my turn. I sat down and talked with Ed, explaining the complaints of the men and the legalities that required us to take this action. Then I issued Ed his withdrawal card in person.

Ed, of course, took the whole thing very personally, feeling that I was really the one behind the members' demands. That could not have been further from the truth. I was simply carrying out the vote of the membership. Ed had been required to do the same thing earlier to Hugh Marionneaux, and so now I had no choice but to do the same thing, even though he was my brother.

Soon, however, another article appeared in the newspaper stating that Ed was denying that the Teamsters had informed him of his ouster. That, too, was a lie. I had gone myself, taken two other Teamsters with me, and personally made it all clear to my brother. But the careful steps I took to try to keep Ed from being hurt did not work. Right there in the prison, he threw a proverbial fit.

Since he had the attorney, Gordon Pugh, there, Ed started building a case that he had been on nothing more than a leave of absence from the local. That argument ignored the facts that Teamsters headquarters

Ed Works Against Me from Prison

had *told* me to issue Ed the withdrawal card, and that the Local #5 members were getting angry to the point of a big uprising over this. And I couldn't blame them; they were right.

I hated doing this more than anyone. Ed was my brother. But no explanation I gave Ed stopped him from coming down hard on me that day.

In another newspaper article, Ed insinuated that he wondered why I had done this him and that he didn't want to name the person responsible for it all. Sometimes Ed didn't make a whole lot of sense. Of course he was talking about me, but that wasn't clear. For my part, I only did what I was required to do by the constitution of the Teamsters, the vote of the local members and the insistence of Teamsters headquarters.

Anyone could see what Ed was trying to do; he wanted to turn the Teamsters membership against me. For me, this was not a problem. I was a big boy now, and I could handle my own business. There was an election coming up, an election in which I would be running for Secretary-Treasurer/Business Manager, the same position I was holding temporarily in Ed's absence. Ed, for his part, was trying everything he could possibly think of to make sure that I lost that election. In the end, I won.

From My Brother's Shadow

Later, in another interview Ed gave from prison, he talked about how he would fight to regain control of Teamsters Local #5. He spoke about being betrayed by fellow Teamsters. He blamed me for things that he said hurt his chances for parole from prison and said that I could not handle the job of Business Manager for Local #5 (even though I had now been in that position for the past year and a half because of his incarceration). This was all just Ed being Ed. I knew in my heart that I had done nothing to deliberately hurt my brother.

If anyone should have been hurt by all of this, it was I. Ed was doing everything he could to get rid of me, after he, himself, had been the one to put me in charge in the first place. I honestly and truly do not know what his problem was. He had always been that way, and he would never change. It was because of Ed that I was in the Teamsters, and I intended to do the best I could for the organization while I was still there.

CHAPTER 11

TEN PERCENT ALIVE BUT NINETY PERCENT DEAD

Ten percent of the time Ed wanted me alive, but ninety percent of the time, he wanted me dead. Ten percent of the time he wanted me alive because he needed my help, and all my life I had helped him every way I possibly could, but that was never enough for him. And so the other ninety percent of the time he wanted me dead. I had somehow become a threat to his future plans.

Through the years, Ed hurt me more than anyone will ever know, but he was still my brother, and I loved him through it all. Although some may choose not to believe it, what I am about to tell you is the truth.

During Ed's reign as boss of Teamsters Local #5 there had been that incident involving a former Local #5 president. That former president had been sent to prison and, as a result of that imprisonment, Ed had been required to cut off his salary. Years later, Ed himself had gone to prison, but of course, Ed being Ed, he wanted to continue being paid *his* salary while he was incarcerated. But this was against Teamsters law. To be paid a salary, a Teamster must prove that he is actually working. Because Ed was still receiving his salary while in prison, a Teamster filed charges against the local. As a result of those charges, I was required to cut off Ed's salary.

This, again, was very traumatic for me, and you can imagine how upset it made Ed. He was *so* upset that he actually put out several contracts on my life — to take care of me permanently. Yes, Ed did that to his own brother. The U.S. government (the FBI) saved me from being assassinated twice that I knew about.

Our phones were tapped, and I can only suppose it had something to do with Ed. Authorities might have had me under surveillance to see if I would manage the affairs of Local #5 in the same manner

Ten Percent Alive but Ninety Percent Dead

Ed had. I never really knew for sure why they were tapped. Anyway, because the FBI had our phones tapped, they were able to record a conversation between some of the people who worked at the union hall and those who were supposed to "do the job" for them. The FBI then tipped me off about the planned attempt on my life, so when the proposed assassins arrived at the hall to take care of me, I was ready for them and got the drop on them, so to speak.

The intended assassins were a Teamsters member and his wife, and they came waltzing into my office one day with the intention of killing me. Fortunately for me, the FBI had done its work, and so I was ready for them.

When they entered, I was sitting at my desk, with a handgun in one hand concealed under a newspaper on top of the desk and a 12-gauge shotgun loaded with double-aught buckshot in the other hand under the desk. Both guns were pointed at the two of them.

The Teamster had his wife's purse over his shoulder, and I could see the butt of a gun sticking out of the purse. He started to reach into the purse, and when he did, I calmly and politely informed him that I had two guns pointed at him. I instructed him to take his gun out of the purse by the butt, very slowly, and lay it on my desk. He did exactly as I instructed him to do, and I emptied the shells from his gun. I then had two Teamsters escort the man and his wife out of the union hall.

When I had been informed by the FBI about that particular attempt on my life, I asked them point blank if there weren't something they could do to prevent it. If they knew he was coming to my office to kill me, why wasn't he going to be stopped? They told me they couldn't do anything unless he actually made an attempt to kill me. In that case, they could act. They said it wasn't against the law to threaten to kill someone; only to act on that threat. That was just one of several such attempts.

Local #5 was looking for a larger building to purchase, and there was a particular building that some Teamsters wanted me to look at. I agreed to take a look at the building, and was making plans to do so ... until the FBI tipped me off and warned me not to go look at that building. At the time, they didn't really tell me why. I found out later. Two people with very bad intentions had been waiting for me at the building. They had a fifty-five gallon drum of acid, and their plan was to kill me and put my body in that drum full of acid.

Ten Percent Alive but Ninety Percent Dead

There was a third plan to kill me that I can now tell about. My wife Sandy and I have in our possession a tape recording of the conversation revealing that plan. The tape was turned over to us by a fellow Teamster. The plan was to shoot me as I drove out of Sandy's driveway. On the tape you can hear the words, "Pop him as he drives out of the driveway, and go on about your business like nothing happened."

These are the details of several of the attempts to assassinate me. Believe them or not, it's the truth. The saddest thing about it all to me was that my own brother was behind them. It was Ed and his people who were setting up these assassination attempts on my life.

To my knowledge none of Ed's family was involved in these plots, but Ed had a lot of contacts, and many of them were with ruthless people. For instance, he was close to Carlos Marcello and other members of the mob in New Orleans. There was a man from New Orleans, known to be one of Carlos' men, who would come by the local office in Baton Rouge once a month to pick up an envelope. But after Ed went to prison, and I took over his duties with the union, that man stopped coming. He never spoke to me, and we never saw him around the hall again.

From My Brother's Shadow

Ed was angry because I had cut off his salary, and he was just doing what everyone called "taking care of business" or "payback." It didn't matter to him that I was family. He would literally run over someone, anyone, to get what he wanted. And he would do anything — whatever it took — to win. Ed didn't care who or what was involved, who got hurt or who died or didn't die. He had a terrible thirst for money and a terrible thirst for power. I don't think anything or anyone ever did or ever could have quenched those two thirsts of his, and that, to me, was very sad.

CHAPTER 12

ED FIGHTS FOR PAROLE

By 1982, Ed was already desperately fighting to be paroled, wanting out of that federal prison in Texas. He had already appealed, and the appeal had been denied. Now there was turmoil brewing in Teamsters Local#5 in Baton Rouge. A big dispute was taking place among the Teamsters members about whether or not to absorb Independent Local 100 (that had seven to eight hundred members at the time).

Ed had promised city/parish officials in 1978 that Independent Local 100 would always remain independent of the Teamsters. But the members of Local 100 had been led to believe, three years before, that they would eventually be accepted into the Teamsters fold. As Secretary-Treasurer/Business Manager, I had been trying to meet that commitment. Ed had not been paying per capita taxes on Independent Local 100 members, and now Teamsters headquarters wanted to know why these taxes had not been paid. It was still up in the air as to whether we might have to go back and pay up all those back taxes, amounting to $5 to $6 a month for each of the Independent Local 100 members over a period of three years.

Unbeknownst to us, Ed had made a deal with some of the city council members that Independent Local 100 members would never be accepted as full members of the Teamsters. They would always remain independent. The problem was that I didn't know Ed had made this deal, and when I found out I was very upset by it. I had promised those members, back when I had organized and signed them up, that they *would* be Teamsters. I would never have agreed with the deal Ed had made, and that's exactly why he didn't tell me about it.

Now, as Ed was working for a parole from prison, a newspaper article appeared in the *State Times* in Baton Rouge. It was dated February 12, 1982, and in the article Ed went from insinuating that Jimmy Hoffa was somehow causing him to remain behind bars, to insinuating that *I* was the one keeping him in prison. He always had to have *someone* to blame for his misfortune. In truth, I did everything I possibly could to gain Ed's freedom. I spoke personally with Louisiana Governor Edwin Edwards (and with anyone and everyone else I could think of), and I wrote letters to the parole board. So that Ed would know about this, I sent copies of the letters to him in prison. He knew what I was doing on his behalf, and yet he tried to make it look as though I was somehow trying to keep him incarcerated. If you read between the lines of everything Ed said and did, you could see that he was trying to show everyone what a sorry son-of-a-bitch I was, in his opinion. Why he thought I would want to keep him in prison I will never know, because he sure as hell couldn't hurt me. There was no way.

Yes, I knew that Ed wanted out of prison. I knew that he was desperate to be paroled, and I would have loved having him out. What brother wouldn't have wanted that for him? But you know what? Ed had been sent to prison by people a lot more powerful than I, and there was nothing I could do about it. Certain people had been trying to put Ed behind bars for years, long before I became principal officer of Local #5.

But let's put all of that aside for the moment and return to the issue of Independent Local 100. I received a letter dated April 2, 1982, from regional and international Teamster official, Mitch Ledet. The letter stated, "I am ordering you to take these people into membership. I have found there was sufficient enough evidence of racial overtones to warrant action by the Teamsters Union."

As I said, years before I had promised these public works employees that they would become full-fledged Teamsters, but now I was the lone figure on the local executive board who supported their absorption. I wanted to do for them what I had promised. The result was that in April of 1982 about eight hundred public works employees became members of Local #5.

But Ed being Ed, he couldn't let it go. Almost a year later he wrote, from prison, a seven-page letter dated March 13, 1983, and addressed to the Teamsters Local #5 membership. Portions of that letter appeared in the *State Times,* dated March 22, 1983. Not surprisingly, Ed criticized the absorption the year before of some eight hundred city/parish public works employees, originally organized as a separate affiliate during his tenure as Boss of Local #5. He stated that he had felt it was better to keep things at a local level, so that those employees would not be subject to pressure from a national union or for a nationwide strike.

That said, let's look back at Ed's struggle for parole. A parole hearing took up this matter on Wednesday, February 10, 1982, in Bethesda, Maryland. The previous year, three national parole commissioners had denied Ed parole, so he had turned around and appealed to the full commission. Ed was not present at this hearing in Maryland, but was represented by two attorneys. After hearing testimony from then Louisiana AFL-CIO President Victor Bussie and from Walter Sheridan, the same U.S. Justice Department official who had worked to bring down Hoffa, a decision was made. Ed had gone to prison in the summer of 1980, facing a possible eight-year sentence for conspiracy to obstruct justice, and his release date had initially been set for May 20, 1986. Now, as a result of the Maryland parole hearing, including the testimonies of Walter Sheridan and Victor Bussie, Ed was scheduled for parole on October 26, 1984. This would have meant he had served fifty-two months in prison.

From My Brother's Shadow

It is possible that Ed's health contributed to this decision. He was said to have been suffering from serious heart problems while in prison, and he was deemed very susceptible to strokes. The reasons for Ed's parole, whatever they were, didn't really matter to me. I was happy for him, that he would be released nineteen months early. I wanted my brother out of jail. I truly did.

CHAPTER 13

THE LOCAL ELECTION OF 1982

Christmas of 1982 was a happy time for me and one I will never forget. Just three days before Christmas, on December 22, I was re-elected by the membership of Teamsters Local #5 as their Secretary-Treasurer/Business Manager, amid charges that I had used unfair tactics to swing the election my way.

Hugh Marionneaux had run against me, but I won the election by a large number of votes. One thousand, four hundred and eighty-two Teamsters took part in that election, and the final tally was nine hundred and twenty-nine votes for me and five hundred and nine for my challenger. Although Ed was still in prison in Texas at the time, he was well aware of what was going on in Baton Rouge.

Hugh protested the results of the election, and on December 30 of that year, contacted local news media and told them all sorts of things. For one, he stated that he had been beaten out of the election by the fact that city/parish workers had been allowed to become members of Local #5. He insinuated that the city/parish workers should not have been allowed to vote, even though they were already full members. And he had other excuses as to why he had lost the election. The truth is that there was a very low turnout that year. Thousands of members had not bothered to vote.

To ensure that the election was fair, I had arranged for actual voting machines to be brought in and used, I believe, for the very first time. No one had to hand-count ballots, so no ballots could be added or taken away. It was a fair and honest election.

Even though Marionneaux lost by a large number of votes, he appealed the election all the way up to Teamsters headquarters. That appeal was denied. He then took his allegations to the National Labor Relations Board and U.S. Department of Labor, and the election was investigated by both agencies. In the end, both agencies determined that the election had been conducted in a fair and orderly fashion.

Part of the problem was that Hugh Marionneaux was associated more with the old timers in the Teamsters, including Ed Partin, and so you can read between the lines on what happened and why.

Marionneaux really wanted very badly to be the secretary-treasurer/business manager of Teamsters Local #5, but I had prevailed in the election, and I had done it without the taint of scandal.

The election was over, I had been re-elected Secretary-Treasurer/Business Manager of Teamsters Local #5, and Ed was still in prison in Texas. I continued to take care of business as I saw fit, as I had been doing ever since Ed had gone to prison and written the note that had originally given me authority to act in his stead. Now, however, there was a difference. I was no longer acting on Ed's behalf; I had been elected to the office on my own, and I took that responsibility very seriously. I was finally out of his long shadow.

From My Brother's Shadow

As always, although Ed was still in prison, he kept very well informed about the business goings-on with the Teamsters in Baton Rouge. And, again, you can read between the lines here. In March of 1983, just months after the election that brought me to power on my own, Jack Arnold, an assistant business agent with Local #5, filed charges against me. Jack had quit his job at the Teamsters hall, and when he quit, he asked me if I would continue to pay his health insurance for the next month so that he could have time to get insurance elsewhere. I agreed to keep his insurance through the Teamsters for one month longer, but no sooner had I done this than Jack turned around and filed charges against me with the union for having done it. Now, you tell me: was that right of him?

Jack had been involved with Hugh Marionneaux and the rest of the group that were opposing me. Now he had the audacity to file charges against me for a favor I had done to try and help him keep his insurance for thirty more days, even though I had the authority to do what I did.

I have in my possession a copy of those charges. They were hand-written on a piece of plain white paper, as follows:

The Local Election of 1982

Charges   March 8, 1983

ART. XIX, SEC. 6, B 3 OF CONSTITUTION PROVIDES:

(1)   Violation — Embezzlement of Union Funds Charges against Sec.-Tres./Bus. Mgr. Douglas Partin

On or about Dec., 20, 1982, Jack Arnold was terminated as Assistant Business Agent of Teamsters Local #5. His insurance was still carried by authorization of Secretary-Treasurer/Bus. Mgr. Brother Douglas W. Partin. This was done without being brought before the present Executive Board. This constitutes a violation of the article stated above because it was being paid out of Local #5's general funds. This also discriminates against other dues-paying members.

I, Francis W. Cramer, do hereby file these charges against Brother Douglas W. Partin on this date, March 8, 1983.

(SIGNED)

_____

From My Brother's Shadow

(SIGNED)

_____

WITNESS: Jack Arnold

(SIGNED)

_____

WITNESS: Deanie Adams

Immediately I knew that Ed was still on top of things from prison — or so it seemed.

In a newspaper article published in the _State Times_ of Baton Rouge, dated March 22, 1983, just days after the charges were filed against me, Ed was quoted as saying, "SOME WANT ME LOCKED UP FOR LIFE." I assume he was referring to me, his own brother. No one _I_ knew of wanted Ed Partin locked up to begin with, especially me.

Ed had been imprisoned for crimes that he committed, not for anything he had done for the Teamsters of Local #5, and not for anything the Teamsters members had done for him or to him. Still, he tried every way in the world he could to get me indicted and/or incarcerated. He wanted me indicted on any kind of charge, he tried to have me killed, and he tried to get the existing Teamsters members to vote against me on everything. Still, nothing he tried worked. The membership had voted for me, and I had been elected.

Shortly after this newspaper article was published, I received a letter from Ed. I still have that letter and also the envelope it was mailed in. The letter read as follows:

Easter Sunday

Dear Douglas:

I just want to know if the people trying to get me indicted feel big on this Easter Day. It doesn't take a man to fight a person in prison. Especially when they are fighting with the police to keep them in prison.
The only thing is, I don't understand why because I was through with the union.

Love, Ed

Try to read between the lines. Ed didn't make much sense sometimes because he had a really screwed-up mind. It didn't matter who had been in control of the Baton Rouge Teamsters; Ed would have hated that person, no matter who it was. And he would have done anything he could to get to that person, just as he was trying to get to me. I really don't know what else I could have possibly done to help Ed, but in the end, it didn't mean anything to him.

Ed caused his own problems. No one put him in prison but himself, by breaking the law. It's as simple as that. He did far too many foolish things and thought he would be able to get away without any consequences, especially after testifying for the government against Jimmy Hoffa. But it didn't work that way.

The federal government had protected Ed as well and as long as they could. They helped him a lot. If it had not been for the federal government, he would have been in some much more serious trouble.

CHAPTER 14

MONEY, MONEY, MONEY

Ed's abuses had gone on for a very long time, and I'm very sorry that things turned out as they did, but they did, and I cannot change the past. Ed was Ed, he did things his way, and he would have to pay the price. His legal problems were not over by a long-shot. I'm telling all of this the way it was, the way it actually happened, from behind the scenes and from his shadow. I'm telling the truth. I was there.

An article from the *State Times* newspaper, published on June 17, 1983, referred to some new racketeering charges. Ed and Allen L. Jones, another Teamster, had both been indicted on federal charges of conspiracy to racketeer and racketeering, as well as three counts of embezzling union funds. The amount of $400,000 was cited in the indictment. The two men were accused of misusing funds from both Teamsters Local #5 and Independent Local 100. The indictment stated that they drew checks on union funds and cashed them at a bank in nearby Denham Springs.

It was also stated that some of the funds had been used to pay Ed's personal state and federal income taxes and that some money had even been taken after Ed had already gone to prison. The indictment further stated that even after Ed was in prison and payments to him had been ordered stopped by an international union official, a $35,000 check for him was drawn on Independent Local 100 funds.

As it turned out, even after I had been in charge, some Teamsters in our local hall continued to funnel money to Ed right under my nose. Ed tried to blame all that on me, but I had nothing to do with it. I didn't send him any money, and I didn't know any money was being sent to him. He was arranging to have that done without my knowledge.

This explains why Ed didn't want Independent Local 100 absorbed into Teamsters Local #5. He wanted to be able to continue to get money out of Independent Local 100 without the rest of us knowing about it.

I had nothing to do with this venture, and I made sure that I had nothing to hide as long as I was in office. Whatever I earned in my paycheck is what I took home, so I had nothing to worry about when it came to accounting for union funds. I can assure anyone of that fact.

What happened to all that embezzled money? Ed and Allen Jones obviously stole the money and hid it somewhere. Then Ed had the gall to blame me for his problems and say that I had wanted him to remain in prison. How in the hell could he blame me, when he was the one stealing money? But you know what? He did.

Amazingly, Ed thought that he could take money from both unions and never be caught. He had grown so accustomed to doing things his way and never having to answer for it that now he didn't know any other way to be.

It was later revealed that Billy Cannon had signed the checks that brought Ed and Allen Jones down. Poor Billy! He just got sucked in by Ed and Allen.

I have in my possession a copy of a check written for the sum of $35,000, made out to E.G. Partin, dated

From My Brother's Shadow

April 9, 1981. It was Check #867 drawn on the account of Independent Local 100. On the check it states that it was for "future contract negotiations." The contract would expire in 1981. This was some of the money involved in the charges against Ed and Allen Jones.

Several newspapers carried articles about this story. Some of the headlines were: JURY PICKED TO DECIDE FATE OF PARTIN AND JONES; PARTIN PLEADS NO CONTEST IN TEAMSTER CHARGES; ED PARTIN PLEADED NO CONTEST AND WAS FOUND GUILTY ON CONSPIRACY, RACKEETERING, AND THREE COUNTS OF UNION FUNDS EMBEZZLEMENT; ALLEN JONES PLEADED GUILTY TO ONE COUNT OF EMBEZ-ZLEMENT. Allen Jones' one-count plea involved the embezzlement of $75,000 of union funds.

When that trial took place, Ed was serving his eight-year term in federal prison. But that was not the end of it. More charges followed, all concerning things which not only happened before Ed's first prison sentence, but also things which happened while he was in prison serving time. Most of the charges Ed faced concerned the mishandling, or outright theft, of money. Money was his problem.

During the time these court proceedings were tak-ing place, I received a little scare myself. A house I owned, located at 5975 Brownfields Drive in Baton Rouge, was severely damaged by fire. Deputies arriving at the scene first reported that the fire had been caused by a firebomb. Thankfully, there were no injuries in that explosion.

I say *explosion* because that was how the neighbors described it. They said they heard a loud explosion and then saw fire. One neighbor reported feeling the blast at her home and getting out of bed after being jolted awake by the explosion.

My son, Donald, who was in a wheelchair as a result of an automobile accident, had been living in that home. The explosion happened on a Wednesday night. The previous Sunday night there had been another fire at the same home, which prompted Donald to move out.

A sheriff's deputy, who, at the time, asked not to be identified, made the comment to a local newspaper that the fires had unnerved many residents of the neighborhood and that if he lived in that neighborhood he would hide behind the bushes with a shotgun. I went by the home that Thursday morning after the fire to check the damage, but I didn't go in because just the sight of it scared the hell out of me.

This fire happened on the eve of the final U.S. grand jury session that had already resulted in indictments against Allen Jones and my brother, Edward Partin. There are questions about the fire incident that I probably will never have answered.

There have been numerous books published over the years about Jimmy Hoffa, the mob, and other related topics, all of which I have read and pondered over. The name of my brother, Edward Grady Partin, appears in them quite frequently. Needless to say, some of the material printed caught my attention because I was there and witnessed things personally. Some people may ask, "Why now? Why are you writing this book now? It's old news. It's like beating a dead horse." But those people don't know me and have never met me. They don't know that I lived and worked in the shadow of my brother for far too many years.

I knew Ed Partin very well, better than anyone else. I saw how he did things, I talked with him, and I worked with him. Ed needed me, so I saw Ed's actions up close. I heard the words he spoke and much more. I probably knew Ed better than he actually knew himself, but because he was my brother, I would not speak until now. I would not reveal the real truth until now. I loved my brother that much.

Many times in the past, reporters, to a certain extent, reported only what Ed wanted them to report, and never the whole story. And what I am revealing here is only the tip of the iceberg, so to speak. There are some things that will never be told, never be heard and never be known. And that is as it should be.

CHAPTER 15

THE MYSTERIOUS DEPOSITION

Much has been made of a certain deposition alleged to have been made by Ed. I knew about that deposition.

I discussed a little in an earlier section about Ed's association with Audie Murphy. Let me go back now to add one more interesting tidbit.

Some have alleged that there was a thirty-one page deposition given by Ed to Audie Murphy, and in that deposition Ed allegedly recanted his testimony against Jimmy Hoffa. Ed had been told that all of his legal problems (of which there were many) would go away if he would cooperate with Carlos Marcello in this matter. And, according to some, Audie Murphy and D'Alton Smith, son-in-law of Carlos Marcello, were assigned to obtain the deposition from Ed.

I can say that Ed did give that deposition. As a matter of fact, he was scheduled to be interviewed at the local Teamsters hall immediately afterward. But, as I mentioned briefly in an earlier chapter, Ed decided not to follow through with the interview. Instead, he sent everyone home and placed a funeral wreath on the door of the hall and a notice stating that our mother had died. It was the middle of the work-week, when everyone should have been working, but the hall was closed. That whole charade was related to the deposition in question.

Ed had agreed to the interview in advance, but something caused him to change his mind, and he invented this elaborate ruse to avoid meeting with the media. When I tell you that Ed Partin would do anything, believe me!

Ed said he had given Smith and Murphy "some words" and that those "words" had been "written down." Ed had hoped that by giving Murphy some type of statement it would help take some of the pressure off of him. In private, he told me that he had actually given them nothing, just "some words." And, although those words, had been written down, he had refused to sign anything.

He said they had accused him of many things, even being involved with the Kennedy assassination. I personally believe that Ed finally told the truth, but then he refused to sign it. So he was able to deny anything they later said against him.

Reportedly, there were several witnesses present when Ed made his statements. Some have claimed that this deposition was then submitted to the parole board, but that consideration for leniency based on the deposition was denied.

The truth is that Jimmy Hoffa had been trying to get Audie Murphy to talk to Ed. Audie Murphy, as a decorated veteran and a well-known movie star, was very well liked. Hoffa was trying every way in the world he possibly could to get out of jail, and he was using Audie Murphy to help him. If Hoffa could have gotten out of jail at that time, he would have gotten right back in the saddle, as far as the Teamsters were concerned. Even if he couldn't have gotten a new trial, he still would have been eligible to lead the Teamsters, but because he was in jail, he couldn't.

I also know that Audie Murphy was trying to help Jimmy Hoffa and that D'Alton Smith, Carlos

From My Brother's Shadow

Marcello's son-in-law, was dealing with Ed, Jimmy Hoffa and Audie Murphy. All of them and all of these events were tied together. Of course, D'Alton Smith and Ed were not on the plane with Audie Murphy when the crash occurred that took Audie Murphy's life.

I have no idea what happened to those deposition documents. Perhaps they are filed away somewhere in a lawyer's office, or maybe they were in Audie Murphy's possession on the plane when he went down. Who knows? It's a mystery maybe never to be solved.

As I sit here thinking about those days, I remember receiving from the federal government in Washington, DC, a list of over a hundred names. I was instructed to go through the list, and if I had talked to, knew, or had dealt with any person on that list in any way, I was to mark the name and explain exactly what my dealings with that individual had been. The list was of mob-controlled and mob-related people around the country.

I went through the list, and I remember thinking that I had to be very careful, because I could have talked to some of those people, not knowing at the time who they were. As it turned out, I didn't know anyone on the list, but I was afraid that, when I had

The Mysterious Deposition

been in a Teamsters meeting in Chicago, New York or some other place, I might have talked to some of them. If I had talked to some of them, not knowing who they were, and now the government knew it, this might cause me some unwanted problems. In the end, I decided to write at the bottom of the list, very specifically, that, as far as I knew, I had not had any dealings with anyone on that list. Carlos Marcello's name was on the list, but I had never met him personally or spoken with him.

Over the years, I was called on to testify many times. I had to appear before a grand jury in New Orleans and a federal grand jury in Baton Rouge, and I gave deposition after deposition to lawyers, simply because I was Ed Partin's brother. When my home in Baton Rouge caught fire and burned, I was required to give statements about that. I've given more darn statements. If someone could go back and check in all those statements that I made in all the various places and to all the various people about the various events, they would find that I told the truth, and there were no contradictory statements.

It's very easy for me to sit here at my desk now and write about things that happened so many years ago, because I know I am telling the truth. I don't have to worry about saying something different than I said on another occasion. As long as I tell the truth, as I know it, and stick with it, there will be nothing to worry about. Of course, there will be those who say I lied or I'm lying now, but that's their problem.

I can tell you this: as I noted at the outset, since I started working on this book, I've had some sleepless nights, for it has brought everything back to me. Reliving some of the past, which I was hoping to forget altogether and forever, has sometimes gotten to me a bit. I wish it had happened differently, but it didn't.

CHAPTER 16

SO MANY OTHER STORIES

There are so many other interesting stories to be told, but there is only so much space in a book. In the years that Ed Partin and I worked together, traveled together and shared so many aspects of our lives, many unusual things happened. Some of them were sad and disappointing to me, but there were also fun and happy times. So here are a few more stories that I'd really like to share with you.

This story is about a prank that our brother Donald pulled on Ed, and every time I think about it, I can't help but laugh. To this day, every time I tell the story, I laugh out loud. I hope it makes you laugh, too.

From My Brother's Shadow

Donald bought a monkey. Yes, an actual live monkey. I can't remember how much he paid for it at the time. This was not a childhood prank; we were all grown men when it happened.

Donald bought the monkey, and then Ed wanted it. He literally begged Donald to sell him that monkey, but Donald refused. I don't know why Ed wanted that monkey so badly, but he did. He even asked me to try to persuade Donald to sell it to him. I decided to stay completely out of the whole matter. Getting between brothers could be dangerous.

As time passed, Ed never gave up. He continued to beg Donald to sell him the monkey. Well, the monkey got sick, and Donald took it to a vet to be examined. The vet told him the monkey was going to die, and there was nothing he could do about it. Donald was a character in his own right, and upon hearing this news, he decided to agree to sell the monkey to Ed.

For his part, Ed was delighted. He finally had his monkey. He had gotten his way again — or so he thought.

Ed took the monkey home, but it wasn't long before he realized something was wrong with it. He took it to the vet, and it just happened to be the same vet Donald had gone to. Seeing that same monkey again, the vet had to inform Ed that he had already told Donald the monkey was sick and going to die, and there was nothing he could do for it. To say the very least, Ed was pissed big time at Donald. The resulting feud lasted a good while between them, but they finally let it go.

Donald and Ed had a somewhat different type of relationship than Ed and I had. If I had been the one selling Ed a sick monkey, he probably would have put out another contract on me.

Throughout this book I've told several stories about Ed and his money. Here are a couple more: As I've stated before, Ed loved his money and always seemed to be able to get his hands on more of it. A movie was made some years ago in which Ed's character was portrayed as not being very well off financially. That was the furthest thing from the truth. When Ed and I and a group of men would sit down in a restaurant to have a cup of coffee or just to shoot the breeze, I couldn't help but notice that the waitresses would all but fight each other to wait on Ed's table. For a long time I wondered why that was. Then one day I learned the secret.

Ed sat at a table alone that day, and he ordered coffee, nothing else. Then, when we all got up to leave, Ed left a hundred-dollar tip on the table for the waitress. Donald saw it, walked past that table, reached down and picked up the hundred-dollar bill and put it in his pocket and replaced it with a one-dollar bill. I imagine the waitress wasn't very happy with Donald that day.

Another time, when Ed and I had gone to a football game in Houston, Texas, he wanted to park as close to the stadium as he possibly could, but there were no parking places close to the stadium available. When we spotted a little gas station near the stadium, Ed drove into the station, pulled out a hundred-dollar bill and gave it to the attendant. As a result, Ed parked at the gas station, and we didn't have very far at all to walk to the ballgame.

Ed did things like that quite often. He would just whip those big bills out of his pocket or go to the trunk of his car and get out a bundle of fresh twenties and amaze everyone. Once, for instance, when he and I were in Arizona, we stopped at a Native American art shop. They had many paintings for sale, and Ed spotted a painting of a Native American on a horse that he really liked. The artist of that work, we were told, was very famous locally and had his own gallery. The asking price for the painting was $10,000. Ed bought it, paying the $10,000 in cash. I saw it with my own eyes.

So Many Other Stories

Besides the painting, that day he also bought two silver and turquoise watch bands and some silver and turquoise rings. He simply went to the car and got the cash money out of the cardboard box he kept in his trunk.

We left the gallery, and as we were driving down the highway, Ed gave me one of the silver and turquoise watchbands as a gift. I didn't want to accept it, but he insisted. I still have that watchband to this day.

Ed always kept money in that box in the trunk of his car. The box was probably about sixteen inches by twenty inches, and he kept it full of twenty-dollar bills that were still in their wrappers. When he needed a little money, he would get a wrapper full of twenties from his car and stick it in his pocket. Whenever he got a little low on money, he would go out to his car and get another wrapper. Ed had money. I know. I was there, and I saw it.

Speaking of Arizona, Ed loved it, and he had a beautiful place in Flagstaff, and went there a lot. I would often be in Baton Rouge taking care of business at the Teamsters hall, and Ed would be living the high life in Flagstaff.

His place in Flagstaff was not far from Las Vegas. You could go up there in the summer, and it was nice and cool, or you could go down to Las Vegas in the winter, and it was nice and warm.

I really don't know if Ed gambled or not. I only went with him to Vegas twice. Let me tell you about one of those trips.

I went with Ed and Sheriff Jessel Ourso of Plaquemine, Louisiana, to a Teamsters convention in Las Vegas. (This happened before Ed went to prison.) We were working hard to get Frank Fitzsimmons elected as president of the International Teamsters Union. Jimmy Hoffa's adopted son, Chuckie O'Brien, had asked us to bring a group of our Teamsters because they were expecting trouble at the convention. He was right.

There were three or four thousand delegates present in the convention hall and another three or four thousand visitors (non-delegates) up in the balconies. A group of Teamsters who were trying to take over the union were very opposed to the election of Fitzsimmons and were disrupting the convention. Ed walked across the convention floor to the troublemakers and tore their microphone off the stand, so that it could no longer be used. As he returned to where we were all sitting, some of the troublemakers followed him. When he realized that they were behind him, he turned around and said, "Now you're in *my* territory!"

So Many Other Stories

I will never forget that day. It was like the wild West all over again. We all had guns (and just about anything else you can imagine) in that convention hall, even though convention security had dogs present supposedly sniffing for both guns and drugs. I'll never forget what one Teamster said after he walked by one of those dogs undetected: "They need to get rid of that son of a bitch! He can't smell shit!"

While at that convention, Chuckie O'Brien gave us Local #5 Teamsters a job to do, an assignment. Our job was to whip a certain person who was running against Fitzsimmons. The International Teamsters Union was having a big party at the Aladdin Casino and Hotel, and our members caught the guy they had been instructed to whip as he was entering the banquet room with a group of other Teamsters. That entire group stayed close together, because they were afraid — and with good reason. But Chuckie O'Brien got what he had asked for anyway: that Teamster, who was running against Fitzsimmons, got the shit beat out of him, and he was carried out of the banquet hall on a stretcher that day.

When one of Fitzsimmons' bodyguards accidentally hit one of our Teamsters (and that son-of-a-gun was supposed to be on our side), all hell broke loose.

From My Brother's Shadow

The bodyguard in question looked like he was at least seven feet tall. One thing led to another, and, when the police showed up, everybody took off running in different directions to hide.

One of our Teamsters was chased down a dead-end corridor. He had a gun on him, but when he sat down on a sofa there in the corridor, he was able to slowly slip the gun under the sofa cushion to conceal it. He was caught and arrested, but they didn't find his gun. We went back later, retrieved the gun, and got him released from jail.

As wild as that was, it was nothing. I mean that was really nothing. I've seen some things go down bad! I mean really bad! This has been one hell of a life.

Now here's another story about Ed and money. Once, when he was trying to make some quick cash, he actually made an arms deal with Fidel Castro in Cuba. He went to Cuba twice and met with Castro both times.

This took place when Ed was still active with Local #5. Now it so happened that he knew a certain Teamster official (I've forgotten what state he was in) who had guns and ammunition connections. Ed called that Teamster and told him he needed some guns. The Teamster asked Ed how many guns he needed. Ed said to him, "I want a big boat, and I want it full of guns and ammunition."

The Teamster asked who the guns were for, and Ed told him they were going to Fidel Castro. "I'm no communist!" the Teamster shouted and hung the phone up on Ed.

That phone conversation took place in Ed's office at Teamsters Local #5, and I tell you what: I was so proud of that Teamster for telling Ed that he was not a Communist and hanging up on him. Ed would have gotten those guns to Castro, if he could have gotten his hands on them. He didn't care. Things like that just did not matter to Ed. All he was concerned about was the money he would make on the deal.

I had served my country proudly in the United States Air Force and the United States Army Reserve and spent time in Korea fighting for freedom. Can you even begin to imagine how I felt hearing that particular conversation? Oh, what a character Ed Partin was!

CHAPTER 17

IMPORTANT REFORMS

As the Teamsters Local #5 elections were nearing in 1985, I had served three good years in the position of Secretary-Treasurer/Business Manager and decided to run for that position again. Ed was still in prison awaiting parole, but, as always, even though he was in prison, he continued to keep up on all the activities in and around Baton Rouge, especially when it came to the activities of Local #5.

The election was scheduled for October 10, and I was confident that the Teamsters members would re-elect me. I was challenged in that election, however, by then Local #5 President Henry Kinchen. Henry and I had worked alongside each other for the past three years. He was a good man and had worked hard for the Teamsters, just as I had.

After I had been elected on my own as principal officer of the local, I had begun making a number of needed changes. I revised the by-laws of the local so that the members would have more power to make decisions and express their will through voting on matters related to the union. My belief was and continues to be that a Teamsters local belongs to its members. It was really their union, and I was working for them.

Before I made those revisions, the members had few choices. They just took what they were given. I had long been a Teamster member myself and had walked in their shoes, and so I knew how they felt. Believe me, I had learned some things, being first on the Teamsters member side of the fence and, then, after being elected as Secretary-Treasurer/Business Manager, suddenly being on the other side of the fence, as the leader of the Teamsters members for whom I worked. As their leader, there were some things I could change, but there were also things that I could not change without the approval of Teamsters headquarters.

My main goal was to create a union owned by the members for whom I worked, giving them a union of which they could be proud. We were able to make some important changes. For instance:

WE CHANGED THE WAY LOCAL #5 ELECTIONS WERE CONDUCTED. State voting machines were brought into the Teamsters union hall and set up by a state official. That person entered the candidates' names and the office each candidate was running for into the machines. That state official, on the day of the election, would open the voting machines for the voting to start and close the machines and tally the votes when the election had ended. No candidate was allowed within one hundred feet of the Teamsters hall while the voting was in progress. Once the voting machines were closed, the candidates were then allowed to observe the state officials as they tallied the votes.

The elections before these new rules were implemented consisted of some Teamsters sitting around with sticks beating on the concrete to intimidate a member before he was given a paper ballot to fill out. After he had voted, his ballot was then placed in a locked wooden box. After the election was over, the locked wooden boxes were taken into an office, and the votes were tallied. Candidates were not allowed inside the office.

From My Brother's Shadow

WE IMPROVED LOCAL #5's MEMBERS' MEET-ING HALL. We installed theater seats bolted to the floor in the members' meeting hall, replacing old folding metal chairs. This was important because the meeting hall was used for any Teamsters meetings, but it was also used on a daily basis for Teamsters members to sit while waiting to be called out on a job.

WE IMPLEMENTED AN OUT-OF-WORK LIST FOR TEAMSTERS TO SIGN IN ON WHEN ENTERING THE UNION HALL LOOKING FOR JOB PLACE-MENT. As strange as it may seem, we had never had a system for those looking for work. It had been handled more on the basis of who found personal favor with whom. Now, when a Teamsters member signed the out-of-work list, he became eligible to go out on a job, and as his name came up on the list, if he was present in the Teamsters meeting room, he could go. If no Teamsters member was present in the meeting room, a phone call was made to the first person on the out-of-work list to go to that job. If a member's name was on the out-of-work list, and a company requested the member by name, he was allowed to go to that job, even though his name was not first on the list.

Important Reforms

WE STARTED A ONCE-A-MONTH NEWSLETTER THAT INFORMED THE MEMBERS OF LOCAL #5 WHAT WAS GOING ON IN THE INTERNATIONAL TEAMSTERS HEADQUARTERS IN WASHINGTON, DC, AS WELL AS IN THE LOCAL. This was long overdue.

WE HAD A COMPUTER SYSTEM INSTALLED WHICH WAS LINKED TO THE INTERNATIONAL TEAMSTERS HEADQUARTERS IN WASHINGTON, DC. It is worthy to note that Local #5 was the last union local to get a computer system linked with the Teamsters headquarters, due to the fact that Ed had never wanted a computer system installed (for obvious reasons).

WE INSTALLED AN 800 NUMBER TO ENABLE THE MEMBERS OF LOCAL #5 TO CALL THE UNION HALL FROM ANYWHERE FREE OF CHARGE TO THEM.

WHEN NEGOTIATIONS WERE HELD WITH ANY COMPANY, I REQUIRED ALL UNION STEWARDS TO BE IN ON THOSE NEGOTIATIONS. THE STEWARDS WERE PAID BY THE LOCAL FOR THEIR TIME SPENT IN THE NEGOTIATIONS AND ALSO

From My Brother's Shadow

FOR LOST TIME ON THEIR REGULAR JOBS. THE STEWARDS WERE ALLOWED TO CALL THE LABOR ATTORNEY REPRESENTING LOCAL #5 ANYTIME THEY NEEDED ADVICE.

WE SENT THE LOCAL #5's OFFICE SECRETARY TO BECOME A NOTARY AND, AS SUCH, SHE WAS THEN QUALIFIED TO BE OF SERVICE TO THE LOCAL'S MEMBERS FREE OF CHARGE.

I WAS ABLE TO CONVINCE SOME AREA CAR DEALERS TO SELL VEHICLES TO THE LOCAL'S MEMBERS AT ONLY $200 OVER DEALER'S IN-VOICE COST.

JOB STEWARDS WERE ELECTED BY THE TEAMSTERS ACTIVE ON JOBS REQUIRING SUCH REPRESENTATION, WITH THE EXCEPTION OF CONSTRUCTION JOBS. THE FIRST MAN SENT TO ANY GIVEN CONSTRUCTION JOB WAS APPOINTED JOB STEWARD BY THE SECRETARY-TREASURER/ BUSINESS MANAGER, AS STATED IN THE LOCAL #5 BY-LAWS. ALL OTHER JOB STEWARDS WERE SENT TO SCHOOL AT THE TEAMSTERS HEADQUARTERS IN WASHINGTON, DC, AND ALL THEIR EXPENSES WERE PAID BY LOCAL #5.

Important Reforms

None of these important measures had been in place before I became principal officer of the Baton Rouge local. During my time in leadership, many other changes were made, but these that I have listed were among the most important to me. I had been elected to lead and work for the members of local #5, and I tried my very best to do what was right for them and give them a union they could be proud of.

After all of this, I was stunned, when, on Thursday, October 10, 1985, I lost the election to Henry Kinchen by fifty-three votes. He had won it fair and square, and as far as I was concerned, that was the end of my Teamsters career. After so many years of being at or near the top, I no longer held any office in the union — although I was still a Teamsters member.

CHAPTER 18

WHAT NOW?

I was nearing my fifty-sixth birthday and had re-married the year before, on April 25, 1984, to Sandra McCraine Wilbert. Sandy worked for the East Baton Rouge Parish School Board, and we had met because I was a good friend of her boss. At one point she thought she might like to work for the Teamsters, but I advised her to stay right where she was. In time, we fell in love and decided to get married.

Now, however, the loss of my position in the union forced the two of us to face some serious changes in our lifestyle. In some ways, we welcomed these changes, but in other ways they were very difficult.

From My Brother's Shadow

I had been married to the union for many long years, and now suddenly I was taking early retirement? My union benefits were not enough for us to live on, so Sandy continued to work at the school board, and I spent the weekdays alone at our camp in Mississippi. It wasn't the best arrangement for newlyweds.

So that I would not be cut off entirely from people, she got me interested in going to flea markets, and we worked with a group of couples displaying some wares here and there. It was a lot of fun.

In 1986 an article appeared in a Jackson, Mississippi, newspaper. It appeared that Ed, Baton Rouge's old Teamsters boss, was now in a Mississippi halfway house. No dates were given as to when he had been released from the federal prison in Ft. Worth, Texas, or how long he was scheduled to remain incarcerated in the halfway house in Mississippi.

Looking back, he had led the Teamsters Union Local #5 in Baton Rouge for more than thirty years. Then he was sentenced, in 1980, to eight years in prison for conspiracy to obstruct justice. He was indicted again in 1983, while still incarcerated on the previous charge, on charges of conspiracy, racketeering, and embezzlement of union funds. In 1984, he had pleaded no contest to those charges and received one six-year sentence and three five-year sentences, all to run concurrently with the original eight-year sentence he was already serving. Now, he was in a halfway house in Mississippi. It was suggested that his health had deteriorated while in prison, making more reasonable his move to the halfway house and his eligibility for parole.

Other than Ed's move to the halfway house in Mississippi, 1986 and 1987 were fairly uneventful and quiet. Sandy and I were living a pretty normal day-to-day life, minding our own business ... until Ed (and a stream of other Teamsters) started coming around, trying to talk me into running for re-election as Secretary-Treasurer/Business Manager of Local #5 in the upcoming 1988 elections. For a while our little road in Mississippi looked like an interstate.

Can you believe it? After all we had been through, Ed wanted me to run again. I was enjoying the more quiet lifestyle and didn't know if I wanted to get back into that stressful situation, and Sandy didn't want me to go back to that for sure. But, as you might have imagined, Ed eventually got his way, and I ran in that upcoming election. The election took place on December 6, 1988, and the results were as follows:

ELECTION RESULTS

6 DECEMBER 1988

PRESIDENT:
1.   DONALD McLEAN ------------------- 248
2.   WILLIAM 'WHIP' WILSON---------- 164

VICE-PRESIDENT:
3.   ALBERT LOPEZ --------------------- 252
4.   RANDY MCNEMAR ------------------ 151

SECRETARY-TREASURER/BUSINESS MANAGER
5.   BILLY BROWN ------------------------ 17
6.   JAMES BROWN, SR. ---------------- 109
7.   JOHN DEPHILLIPS ------------------- 73
8.   HENRY KINCHEN--------------------- 67
9.   DOUGLAS PARTIN ------------------ 189

There had been a total vote count of about 663 in the 1985 election, in which I lost by about 53 votes. In the 1988 election, a total of 435 votes were cast, and 189 of the votes put me back in office. I had been returned to the post of Secretary-Treasurer/ Business Manager of the Teamsters Union Local #5, but, alas, I was in for a great shock.

What Now?

I am looking at a letter dated 20 January, 1989, and originating from the desk of J.W. Morgan, Teamsters International Director. It was addressed to me, Mr. Doug Partin, and signed by Charles H. Jones, Secretary-Treasurer. The letter was sent by certified mail (#P973 524 759). It stated:

YOUR PER-CAPITA TAX TO THE SOUTHERN CONFERENCE OF TEAMSTERS FOR THE MONTHS OF OCTOBER, NOVEMBER AND DECEMBER HAS NOT BEEN RECEIVED IN THIS OFFICE … . PLEASE LET US HAVE YOUR PER-CAPITA TAX PAYMENT SO THAT YOUR LOCAL UNION WILL BE IN GOOD STANDING AND YOUR MEMBERS WILL NOT BE DENIED BENEFITS.

As soon as I received that letter, the cleanup began. Teamsters Union Local #5 was in pretty bad shape financially, and I was facing a great challenge to put things right. It may seem strange to some, but I welcomed this challenge. I had been in the union long enough that I had the confidence I could turn things around.

There is another interesting document from that same period. I'm not sure of the exact date of it. It

From My Brother's Shadow

was evidently the minutes of a short meeting we held to begin to face this challenge. It was handwritten on a plain piece of paper and read as follows:

Doug Partin
Donald McLean
Albert Lopez
John Miller
John Levigne
Lenwood Stilley
Lawrence Guillot

MEETING CALLED TO ORDER BY
DONALD McLEAN

DUE TO THE ECONOMICAL CONDITIONS
OF THE LOCAL, MR. DOUG PARTIN
WILL RECEIVE NO SALARY UNTIL SUCH
TIME AS THE LOCAL CAN AFFORD TO
PAY. THEN THE SALARY WILL BE PAID
RETROACTIVE TO 28 DECEMBER 1988,
SALARY TO BE $770.00 PER WEEK.

JOHN MILLER MADE A MOTION TO
AUTHORIZE DOUG PARTIN TO POST
NOTICES ON ALL JOBS ADVERTISING
FOR BIDS ON THE 1987 COUGAR CAR

What Now?

FOR SALE, WHICH BELONGED TO THE TEAMSTERS UNION LOCAL #5 WHEN HENRY KINCHEN WAS IN OFFICE.

SECONDED BY DONALD McLEAN
MOTION CARRIED UNANIMOUSLY.

SIGNED:
JOHN MILLER
ALBERT LOPEZ
JOHN A. LEVIGNE
DONALD H. McLEAN
LAWRENCE GUILLOT
LEON LENWOOD STILLEY, SR.

Contrary to what some may have believed, I cared about and was devoted to Teamster Union Local #5, and I worked some long and hard hours without pay in order to get things back on track after being re-elected in 1988. I think these minutes of the meeting should prove that fact to any doubters.

I worked for the next seven months with no salary and was able to pay off $80,000 in bad debts left behind by my predecessor. Once the local was again financially secure, I reinstated salaries for the business agents and myself. Those salaries were fair and equal and were in force until I retired in 1994. Salaries ranged from $45,000 in 1988 increasing to $50,000 in 1994. Once again, the local was marching along well and fulfilling its purpose of serving the working men and women of the Baton Rouge area.

CHAPTER 19

THE END OF AN EPOCH

1990 was not a good year for the Partin family. Ed had been out of prison for a good while, but not much had been heard from him, either publicly or in the news. He was spending most of his time in the McComb and Brookhaven, Mississippi, areas. I'm sure he must have traveled to other places, but my personal knowledge is limited in this regard. After convincing me to run again, Ed was back to his old tricks, and I didn't hear much from him.

I don't know if Ed ever had a home to call his own after his incarceration or not. Only his immediate family can answer that question. He was said to have often traveled with a companion, but I never knew who it was.

Edward Grady Partin was a mysterious man and had lived a life of intrigue, danger, excitement, duplicity, and voracity, and yet he was still loved, looked up to, and cherished from his shadow, by a younger brother. That was me — Douglas Westley Partin. As difficult as it may be for some of you who are reading this to believe, this is SO TRUE! BELIEVE ME!

In the latter part of January, 1990, it was reported that Ed was near death in a Florida hospital. At 65, he was suffering from heart disease and diabetes, and had been removed from all life support systems and taken off of all but pain medications. He was moved to a private room in a Baton Rouge nursing home to allow family members to spend time with him before his passing. Sandy and I, along with many others, paid our last respects there. He died there on Tuesday, January 23, 1990.

Somehow I think that Ed died wishing me dead instead, but I wished him no ill will and had just left him before he breathed his last. Some of his children were with him when he died, and he loved having them around. His lungs had filled with fluid, and there were no doctors there in the nursing home to attend to him as he breathed his last.

Sadly, Ed died with some very bad feelings. Just days before he died, he told those around him that I had stolen $40,000 from him, and he also accused others of doing the same. I don't know why Ed did or said the things he did. I would never have stolen anything from him. I think he just wanted to leave some mystery behind.

It is noteworthy that Ed also had some of the Teamsters around him in that nursing home. Three or four stayed close-by at all times. They had loved him and always called him BOSS! Now they hovered over their BOSS in his last moments of life.

It was one of the Teamsters who told me what Ed had said about me stealing the $40,000 from him. What a big lie that was!

But that was Ed. He just had to do something attention-grabbing, as he sensed that he was dying. He wanted to leave the Teamsters thinking that I had stolen from him. Ed would do anything, and nothing bothered him. I'm convinced that it never crossed his mind that anything he had ever done was wrong — even as he lay on his death bed facing eternity.

From My Brother's Shadow

In truth, Ed had never enjoyed the best of health, and through the years, he used that fact in any way that would benefit him. Once, in Houston, Texas, he went to a hospital rather than keep a court date. Of course, he made sure his car was parked so that he could see it well from his hospital window. After all, he kept that big cardboard box of money in the trunk.

Every time the doctor was about to discharge Ed, his temperature would go sky high. Eventually the doctor caught on to the fact that Ed had found a way to make his temperature rise at will. The next day, he discharged Ed, accusing him of faking his illness.

And he was right. Ed was something!

Even though he sometimes did not enjoy good health, Ed had been a strong man in other ways, and many adored him. Now an epoch had come to an end. It was a pivotal point in the history of the Partin family and in the history of the Teamsters Union Local #5 in Baton Rouge, Louisiana.

Suddenly the shadow of Edward Grady Partin was no longer, and, for me, life went on, work moved forward, and the leadership of the Teamsters Union Local #5 and its membership continued. I had grown in my profession through the years, and now

The End of an Epoch

I was able to lead, in a very professional manner, the Teamsters Union and it members to whom I felt total loyalty and dedication.

In the days and months that followed, issues such as the following were going on in the Baton Rouge, Louisiana, area:

- FIREFIGHTERS VOTED TO ACCEPT A NEW PAY PLAN.
- THE METRO COUNCIL APPROVED A NEW PAY PLAN FOR ALL CITY/PARISH EMPLOYEES.
- THE TEAMSTERS UNION LOCAL #5 MEMBERS APPROVED A NEW THREE-YEAR CONTRACT WITH THE CITY/PARISH GOVERNMENT.
- THE AREA'S UNION GROWTH WAS STABLE.

Time marched on ... until the 1991 Teamsters Union Local #5 elections neared. I decided to throw my hat into the ring and run for a third term as Secretary-Treasure/Business Manager of Teamsters Union Local #5, and the results were positive:

From My Brother's Shadow

1991 TEAMSTERS UNION LOCAL #5 ELECTION RESULTS

DOUG PARTIN ------------------------- 300

ALLEN 'BOOTSIE' JONES ----------- 58

I had been re-elected again and given yet another chance to lead the Teamsters of the Baton Rouge area for the next three years. Now, the normal day-to-day, week-to-week, and month-to-month duties I was elected to perform provided the newspapers with no sensational articles about Teamsters Local #5 to print. And that was just fine with me. Things were going pretty smoothly for me professionally, as I prepared for my retirement at the end of that term in office.

CHAPTER 20

MY RETIREMENT

In time my retirement letters were written, and I think they express well the culmination of my leadership of Teamsters Union Local #5. The first letter, dated June 3, 1994, was addressed as follows:

General Executive Board
International Brotherhood of Teamsters
25 Louisiana Avenue, NW
Washington, DC 20001

Dear Brothers and Sisters:

For the past forty-five years, except for time spent in the Army during the Korean Conflict,

I have been a member of Teamsters Local #5 and the International. I now come to the end of the road and will not seek re-election this fall.

I would like to thank all of the Members of the General Executive Board, General President Ron Carey, and General Secretary-Treasurer Tom Sever for the cooperation they have given Local #5 in the past two (2) years. You have answered promptly every call that has been made upon you for your services. You have performed the most difficult tasks and made many personal sacrifices on behalf of our Union.

Thank you for the courage and devotion you have shown in sticking to your posts and the jobs you were elected to do in the face of so many reasons to retreat.

If I do not have a chance to see you before I retire, I would like to say I'll miss you. It is my hope that you will continue to give your services to this great Union and be blessed with good health for many years to come.

Fraternally,
Doug Partin

My Retirement

Secretary-Treasurer
Business Manager DP/fw

Cc: Each Executive Board Member
Ron Carey, General President
Tom Sever, General Secretary-Treasurer

I was very excited about my upcoming retirement and about spending more time with Sandy on our property in Mississippi.

On 17 January 1995, I received a letter of great importance to me.

Mr. Douglas W. Partin
517 Perrytown Road
Crosby, MS 39633

Dear Brother Partin:

The Trustees of the Teamsters Affiliates Pension Plan are pleased to inform you that your application for a Retirement Pension has been approved.

Therefore, you will receive a monthly pension, effective January 1, 1995, in the amount of $968, payable for your lifetime. One-half of this amount will be payable for the lifetime of your spouse in the event your spouse survives you. If your spouse should predecease you, you have the right to change your benefit to the 60-Month Guaranteed Annuity amount. The initial payment will be mailed to you in the near future. Commencing approximately February 1995, your payments should be electronically transferred to your bank on the first business day of the month.

The actual amount of you benefit differs slightly from the previously estimated amount, since the earnings verified by Local Union #5 for the year 1982 differ from those that were previously reported to the Administration Office and which were used for the estimate. If you have any questions concerning this determination, please contact the Administration Office.

We wish to take this opportunity to express our appreciation to you for your service on behalf of an Affiliate of the International Brotherhood of Teamsters.

With the business of my retirement taken care of, there was one more letter that I wrote. It was sent to the news media and industries, politicians and all the members of Teamsters Union Local #5:

END OF THE ROAD

Upon my forthcoming retirement, I would like to address the following groups:

To the many industries on the river and in the Baton Rouge area: I would like to thank you for the thousands of jobs you have given the members of Teamsters Local #5. It is with deep regret that I acknowledge that positions taken in the past by many labor leaders, including myself, did not gain support from the public nor industry for union labor.

To the Louisiana politicians, both past and present: It has been a privilege to have known you. Many of you have served the citizens of Louisiana faithfully and honestly. I am grateful to you for the public service you have performed, even though I have disagreed with your vote on many occasions. You have served your constituencies well.

From My Brother's Shadow

To the citizens of Louisiana: I will miss you most of all. Where else in this country can you find such a rich and wonderful culture?

To the thousands of Teamsters whom I have had the privilege of knowing over the past forty-five years: I would like to thank you for your loyalty and for the sacrifices you have made for this union, my brother Ed, and me. I owe you my affection, gratitude, and respect. God bless you, and carry on.

Sincerely,

Doug Partin
Secretary-Treasurer
Business Manager

Even in my final letter, I was still thinking of my big brother, Edward Grady Partin, whom I loved so very much.

CHAPTER 21

NEW HURTS

Some years have now passed, and I sit in my home office going through some of my notes pertaining to my time with the Teamsters in Baton Rouge. After I resigned my post, I helped my nephew, Keith Partin, Ed's youngest son, get elected as the new principal officer of Local #5. I continued as a Teamsters member, and in that capacity I attended an interesting meeting. of which I have some notes. The meeting was held on May 20, 1996.

According to my notes, a previous union meeting had been held, and a vote had been taken to pay me back salary for the months I had worked without pay to get the local out of the red. This second meeting on the issue was conducted by Keith himself. I noted:

DOUG: "Keith, Can I ask you a question?"

KEITH: "Yes!"

DOUG: "What I don't understand, Keith. How is it that you deny a person who came to the local and worked seven months without a pay-check, under the pretense that when this local got in good shape, they would pay him back his money? Now, I worked for seven months. I worked my butt off up here without a dime, and the Executive Board agreed they would pay me when they got the money. Now, you mean to tell me these members would deny a member the money he worked for and he deserved his back pay that he was supposed to get?

I'm not saying I have to get it all now. I'm just saying that what you are doing is wrong, Keith! If you came up here and worked for seven months, you're entitled to be paid, Keith! We didn't have money to operate. I had to pay the light bill for the union hall out of my own pocket! We didn't have money to do anything. They were about to turn the telephones off! We had to scrounge up money to pay the telephone bill. We were $80,000 in debt the day we walked in the door. We left you, what, thirty or $40,000 in the bank."

KEITH: "$24,000!"

DOUG: "Okay, we left you $24,000 in the bank. When we walked in here, we owed $80,000, and you mean to tell me now you want to deny me what I worked for as a union man? You wouldn't do that to a man working out there on a job! You would be jumping over this building trying to get the man his money! I can't believe any member of this local would do that! I DON'T BELIEVE IT!"

KEITH: "Doug, things work different!"

DOUG: "OH! OKAY!"

KEITH: "Not a year and a half down the road, after I came in here. Sure, there was $24,000 in the bank, and now there's $46,000."

DOUG: "Good! That's great, and I'm proud of you. It's not $80,000 in debt, is it? That's where we were, $80,000 in debt."

The meeting went on and on like that, and in the end, I was not granted my back pay. I had worked and earned that money, but I never received the back pay for which I had worked so hard!

Then, on October 10, 1996, Keith issued me a withdrawal card from Teamsters Union Local #5, which he himself signed. There was no reason for him to do this. I was a retired Teamster drawing a retirement pension and absolutely no threat whatsoever to my nephew in his position.

I was very disappointed and hurt that Keith felt he had to do such things to the uncle who had hired him at the Teamsters union hall and had later worked hard to help him get elected to succeed me in that position. Receiving that back salary was a factor in the calculations for my retirement benefits, and not receiving it hurt.

In time, I was able to mend fences with my nephew, Keith, and every now and then he calls or comes to see me for advice. I want him to do well and be a good and fair leader of Teamsters Union Local #5.

I have always been a very caring and forgiving person. I enjoy life. I love and laugh, and am a very happy and contented person, even after all I've had to endure in life. I like people and will always be there for a friend or family member in need of help or advice.

CHAPTER 22

MY REGRETS

Although I am proud of my accomplishments in life, there are obviously things that I am not proud of, things that I regret. Through the years, I was not an angel by any means, and I did things that I've had to learn to live with.

Many of the things I did during my Teamster years were done because I honestly felt at the time that they were the right thing to do. I was Ed's brother, and he was my boss. But I was not Ed in any sense of the word, and people eventually came to know me for myself. I was always and will always be Ed Partin's younger brother, and there's nothing I can do to change that fact, but I am not Ed. I am Doug.

From My Brother's Shadow

As I am thinking back now, an old saying that I have heard all my life comes to mind. I've heard people say, "If I had my life to live over, I wouldn't change a thing." Well, if I had the chance to live my life over, there are a *lot* of things I would change, believe me.

One thing I would certainly change is the trouble I got myself into when I was sixteen and I stole that Cushman motor scooter. If I had that to do over, it would never have happened. It was wrong, and if I could go back and correct it, I would.

Another thing that has haunted me my whole life and something I think about all the time is this: When I was a teenager, and we were living on Union Street in Natchez, there was a couple (I think their last name was Smith) who lived one street over on Rankin Street. I think it was the 600 block of Rankin. That couple had a son about my age, and he was a good kid. Together they made a really nice family. Back then, everyone was growing Victory Gardens, and I can't explain why I did it (to this very day, I don't understand why I did it myself), but I went over to their house and tore up their Victory Garden.

I never forgot it, and it is something I will always regret. I did it. I admit that I did it, and it was so wrong. It should never have happened.

My Regrets

I have told much here, and yet many there are other details of my life that are not covered in this book. Even now, I sit here pondering the past and anguishing over what facts I should include and what facts I should leave for a future time.

There are many people this book will anger. There are family members of friends and former business associates, who have gone on before me, that I do not want to hurt in any way. If anyone is hurt unintentionally, I am truly sorry for that. But these things needed to be told.

I have taken great care and preparation to insure that more of the details of my life will one day be disclosed. There are audio tapes, which I personally recorded, as well as other items of interest that are to be turned over to the proper media outlets upon my death. Then and only then will my life become a totally open book. Perhaps then everyone will better understand my past actions and words.

Well, we are coming to the end now. I intended to write a book about my life, but now that it's finished, it may seem to some to be more like a book about my brother Ed. For so many years, I lived in his shadow. My life and his life were so intertwined that at times it was difficult to separate the two. Ed received such attention and notoriety during his

From My Brother's Shadow

lifetime that just the fact that I had the same last name automatically associated me and my family with him — whether we liked that or not.

Because I lived in Ed's shadow and worked in his shadow for so many years, I was known to many people simply as "Ed's brother." That was hard to escape, but, as I have shown here, I was eventually able to step out of his shadow and prove myself for who I was, to stand on my own two feet and to live by my own convictions, not Ed Partin's.

Well, that's what my life was like ... so far at least. Tomorrow is another day. Thank God I'm free *From My Brother's Shadow.*

Index

From My Brother's Shadow

B

C

Index

N

Index

From My Brother's Shadow

W

Y

CONTACT
INFORMATION

You may contact the author at:

Douglas Westley Partin
517 Perrytown Road
Crosby, MS 39633
Phone: 601-639-4802

OR

22514 Tucker Road
Zachary, LA 70791
Phone: 225-301-8135